STORMS PASS, SO HANG ON!

Denise 803-365-1260
at
Work
Patterson 1-800-544-3571 1340
1791
1

1-800-658-8978
Natural Cures
Berr

STORMS PASS, SO HANG ON!

Nancy Hoag

Beacon Hill Press of Kansas City
Kansas City, Missouri

Unless otherwise indicated, all Scripture quotations are taken from the *Holy Bible, New International Version®* (NIV®). Copyright © 1973, 1978, 1984 by International Bible Society. Used by permission of Zondervan Publishing House. All rights reserved.

Permission to quote from other copyrighted versions is acknowledged with appreciation:

The *Revised Standard Version of the Bible* (RSV), copyrighted 1946, 1952, © 1971, 1973.

The Living Bible (TLB), © 1971 by Tyndale House Publishers, Wheaton, Ill.

American Standard Version (ASV).

King James Version (KJV).

10 9 8 7 6 5 4 3 2 1

For the man who was there to hold my hand, the man who brought warm milk, hot soup, and laughter—who tucked the blankets up and built the fire warm—the man who listens even when I am not exactly certain I know what I'm talking about.

The man who's teaching me to relax and to play, who's learning with me how to wait.

For my husband, my friend.

Contents

*At times God puts us through
the discipline of darkness
to teach us to heed Him.*
—OSWALD CHAMBERS

Prologue

"Though he brings grief, he will show compassion, so great is his unfailing love. For he does not willingly bring affliction or grief to the children of men" (Lam. 3:32-33).

Twice in one week, I'd been asked for my telephone number, and twice I didn't know. One woman was so kind—asked me if maybe I could just remember the area code for either my present home or the last—then she'd look up my file. My area code? "I've overloaded, that's all," I told myself. Besides, I'd become a grandmother twice. Grandmothers aren't supposed to remember everything, are they? And we'd moved again—7 homes, an apartment, our daughter's basement, numerous motels—in less than 17 years. Three of those homes, the apartment, our daughter's basement, motels—all in the last 36 months. Yes, I was waking up some mornings wondering, for a second or two, which house? Where? But, this was normal, right?

I'm a strong person. Just this morning a Christian friend who's known me for decades remarked that most people see me as in control, bright, cheery, nothing I can't handle, nothing bothering me. But they don't know me— not the me my friend knows, not the me my spouse lives with. And what about God? Surely He knows me even better than I know myself.

In the beginning, I thought all this moving around was great fun! A chance to see new sights, meet new people, decorate yet another home. But then, one day two moves ago, I began to lose it.

A former pastor wrote of "the dark winter of the soul that you have been experiencing," pointing out I was "tired, angry, confused, and full of fear." He was right. I'd gotten very tired of the moving. Angry? Yes! Confused? Well, I'd believed God had told me to write, but now it

11

seemed we'd made two moves too many, and I'd shut down. Full of fear? That, too—when I asked myself what I planned to do with the rest of my life. "I'm barely into my 50s!" I'd counted on at least 50 years more.

When did it begin, my coming to the end of myself, the journey that would take me not only across country, back, and across country again, but to a place where I would discover I wasn't nearly as strong as I'd once thought—to a place where I would discover, apart from God, I would never be well? Yes, a couple of years ago I'd typed a card, placed it on my bulletin board, prayed the same prayer every day for months: "Lord, let the things that restrict me be removed." But hadn't He removed not what restricted me but what I *needed* and *couldn't* give up: old friends, a familiar land, roots? There'd been a surgery, envy, an estrangement from my son. I'd been disconnected from colleagues, cut off from a world I loved. Worse, I was losing my sense of self.

God says in His Word He has known me (and you) since before we were placed in our mothers' wombs. You know what else? He says He knows our *hearts!* Oh, sure, He sees the good we *desire* to do—but He also sees pride, anger, fear, a self that's larger than life, the things that restrict us, things needing to be removed. I've asked Him so many times, "Why another relocation? Why can't we put down roots? Why this? Why that?" Today, I'm thinking, for me at least, the moves have been necessary because I needed not what *we* call "happiness" but contentment— that I might let go of preconceived notions, that I might find my roots in Him.

My former pastor said it was imperative that I reach out, admit I was having trouble and that I was mad! "First, find two people (in addition to Scotty) with whom you can bare your soul, people who love you and will take responsibility for you, burden bearers who will take you on as a ministry." People who would listen and listen and pray—for months, perhaps.

"I can't do that!" I wailed. "I'm an 'inspirational' writer . . . I minister *to* . . . I can't admit . . ."

"You must not just pray for yourself; you must be prayed for," my pastor wrote.

Prayed for? How long would *that* take? I wanted the sun to shine on me *now!* Wasn't it shining on just about everyone else? I needed spring—in Montana, not on the East Coast! Yet, when we lived in Montana, hadn't I whined—found things wrong with "home" too? Hadn't I grumbled, murmured, complained?

Happiness keeps changing the rules on us, keeps moving the goalpost—an ethereal thing. It's contentment we're wanting. Discontentment (which loves to walk with self and pride) is that which shipwrecks us, brings us down. But in the midst of our frustration and bewilderment God *is* faithful.

"You will know when the day breaks and when the night flees away," my pastor wrote. "Fear will give way to confidence. Weariness will be overcome with a new energy." I thought I simply needed to see an end to my waiting, needed spring and needed it now, needed it somewhere else other than this new place we'd relocated to. But I needed prayer. I needed, also, to let go.

I'm not the only one who's been waiting, longing, discontent. A young mother waits for children to grow so that she might return to her art. An older mother waits for her son to graduate from college so that she might also go back to school. A wife waits for her husband's healing and wonders, Where is God? A widow waits, hopes someone will call, come to her door, remember she's spending too much time alone.

I don't know what's keeping you from feeling as if spring has arrived. I don't know what God's doing in your life. But I have learned we *can* become content in whatsoever state. It's a matter of letting God do whatever needs to be done within us—that we might never again look to any*one* or any*thing* but to Him for the joy the spring brings. Winter sets in on our spirits and leaves us feeling as though we, like winter wheat, are about to grow; but then the cold winds we call circumstances (usually, we call them unhappy circumstances or unforeseen or cruel) buffet us into feeling shelved like a book that God's decided not to check out.

Those of you who remember the '50s—remember the air-raid alerts too? Do you remember their announcing, "This is a test, this is only a test"? Well, to those of you longing for spring but discovering, just about the time you've begun to send up your little green shoots, along comes winter, and you're under three feet of snow, and then the rains follow and the storms—to you, I want to say, "This is a test, this is only a test. God is no respecter of persons. What He has done for me—spring, at last and out of the dark—He longs to do for you." Whatever your need, He has it in Him to meet that need; He is your Source of supply.

Before the breakthrough, I remember calling one of my burden bearers, asking her to meet me for coffee, telling her I was empty and didn't believe I'd ever get well. But before we met, she prayed. And as she prayed, she wrote in her notebook reflections the Lord brought to mind: "We must always keep our focus on God and who He is and what He has done, not on what He has withheld." Then she wrote, "Ask God to remove the desire for more and to teach you contentment in all circumstances."

It didn't happen overnight, but healing has come. Today, I'm experiencing contentment, realizing what a good thing God has done. Today I called my friend.

"I feel as if, in my spirit, I could actually somersault!"

I said. "I'm a golden retriever running with her nose through autumn's leaves, tail wagging, chasing squirrels. Free to be what God has planned, free to do what He asks!" I don't mean to sound melodramatic, but this morning I'm sitting in my study in Virginia, which looks out into woods where there are deer, so many birds, and last night, a raccoon. I love the quiet; it's quiet here. The sky's lovely, spring's beginning to show itself in the form of crocuses and daffodils. So what, after all, is my complaint? Are these not gifts from God?

My tests may not resemble yours. For others, similar. But our God, our Father? The same. His love for me, for you? The same. For me, it was depression like a thick, gray fog—waking up mornings and feeling disappointed that I had. But does He love me? Yes, He does. He loves me enough to make me move to where I don't want to go, to leave me where I don't want to stay—that I might learn to become content, period. And, content, will anything seem again too difficult? will circumstances send me into despair?

And, what about you? Will He listen? Will He answer your prayers? Is He watching, caring? Does He know how it will all come out and will it be for your own best good? Yes, if you will simply trust, rest, and accept that *whatever* is coming or has come your way, He has not missed it. He didn't just happen to have His back turned. He knows best, loves best, can handle it all. So, let Him. Hang on to His promises, His Word. Keep your hand in His.

I know whom I have trusted.

Storms pass, so hang on!

I NEED SPRING

He that walketh in darkness, and hath no light, let him trust in the name of Jehovah, and rely upon his God.

ISA. 50:10, ASV

Not Just Another Fish Story

For hours, forecasters had predicted snow. But my husband had assured, "We'll be home *long* before the first flake falls."

It crossed my mind to suggest Scotty's optimism had something to do with his believing some trophy-winning fisherman would be divulging secrets, and he'd catch his limit next time he waded into a trout-filled stream. But I kept my thoughts to myself, and we headed for the sportsman's show and, if my husband's expression was any indication, paradise.

A firstborn perfectionist, I'm not exactly patient. But when my husband grins like a small boy in an apple tree, I give up. In Harrisburg, my husband grinned. He also donned fishing vests, tested duck calls, and swapped jokes with outfitters who'd traveled from Rocky Mountain states. And I—surrounded by bill caps, Stetsons, cowboy boots, and bragging—grimaced over my watch, wondering about the weather reports my spouse had dismissed with a wave of his hand. Not until I'd retreated to a padded bench in an empty RV did Scotty decide five-plus hours was enough. *Finally* we were going home, and was I glad!— glad, that is, until I overheard a highway patrolman saying something about snow falling and falling fast!

"Scotty!" I gripped my husband's hand.

Scotty slipped his arm around my shoulders, grinning. A little snow was "no big deal."

That was inside the auditorium. Outside, my whipped hair wilted and my makeup smeared as I ducked my wet, freezing face to my chest.

"Coffee, Babe?" Scotty asked, as we pulled out of the near-empty parking lot and glimpsed golden arches against an angry sky.

"No!" I snapped. "Thanks," I fabricated, lips stiff.

The snow was becoming more than flurries. Alongside the highway it was beginning to mound.

What in the world did he find so fascinating about that stupid show? I glared out my window as Scotty covered my fist with his warm hand.

"You upset?" he asked.

"No!" I chirped. You've got that right! We'll be lucky if we don't die out here!

"Don't worry, Babe, I grew up in this stuff."

It was true. He'd been raised on a Montana ranch. He'd experienced conditions much worse than these. But I'd grown up with beaches, ferries bobbing across a shimmering sound, and in a place where no one in his right mind challenged this kind of winter storm.

We hadn't been on the Pennsylvania Turnpike long when snow began to cover the glass.

"*Please* stop!" I begged, shelving every promise to be still.

Scotty signaled and entered an exit where garish neon tempted travelers to have one for the road.

"Not *here!*" I shrieked.

"Baby, will you relax?" Scotty shifted down. "There's a diner up the road where we'll eat."

"I don't want to eat!" I hugged my door. Were we sliding?

"Then, why did you—?"

"I want you to stop driving until the snow's gone!" I bawled.

"Babe, come here." Scotty set the brake, offered a hug. I refused.

"There's nothing to worry about."

I wanted to believe he was telling the truth. "OK," I mumbled, allowing one embrace. "But please get us back to the turnpike. I want to go home," I wailed, vowing never again to accompany him to anything having to do with hunting or fishing or those dumb ducks. "Anyone with any sense—"

"Babe . . ."

"OK, I'll be quiet." But this is ridiculous!

Our wills came to mind. Should we have updated them? Would Lisa be happy with the china cupboard? Did Rob still want my desk? And what about Tammy now that she had a piano of her own?

For the next 20 miles, I said *almost* nothing. Nose against my window, I watched for white lines and ravines—and wondered if they'd find us before spring.

"This is the pits," Scotty said. "Sorry, Babe."

I wanted to say it was OK. "I can't believe you did this!" I yelped.

"Shouting won't help!"

"Well, if you'd used your head . . ." My words froze midair.

He'd turned the headlights off.

"What are you doing?"

"Trust me; I can see better this way."

"*Trust* you? *You* wasted our entire day gawking at deer hides *and* deerflies *and* wobblers *and* plugs!"

"Believe me, you won't have to go with me *again.*" He worked his jaw the way he does when he's not yet fed up but close.

"There won't be any again. We'll die out here, and tomorrow they'll read how two idiots were found on the turnpike—engine running and lights off!"

Scotty's jaw clamped.

Will you be quiet? He's doing the best he knows how. "Please turn the lights on," I begged.

He did, but the powerful beams only made matters worse as they bounced off what seemed a wall of snow.

Scotty turned the headlights off again, and I attempted to relax. Now, however, we couldn't tell where one lane ended and another began. Scotty hunched over the wheel, staring. I rolled my window down and bellowed, high-pitched, when he'd wandered too close to the berm. We slowed to a crawl. I touched Scotty's hand. We couldn't go much farther, could barely see beyond the hood. Our Honda wasn't up to plowing drifts.

"Scotty, what will we do?"

"Have you prayed?" he asked.

Too full of I told you so, prayer hadn't crossed my mind. "No," I said.

"Neither have I." Scotty squeezed my hand. "Let's pray, Babe. OK?"

I closed my eyes, hoped my husband hadn't done the same, and, praying, felt peace displace fear.

Asking the Lord's forgiveness for our angry outbursts and hearing Scotty's prayer echo mine, I knew immediately: we weren't alone. Tension withdrew and I released Scotty's hand, squinted sideways, *and* spotted an 18-wheeler pulling alongside and out in front packing snow, blazing a trail.

For the next hour, we focused on three red lamps at the top of the trailer and barely visible taillights on either side. We feared the driver would pick up speed, but he didn't—not until *after* we'd signaled and exited the down ramp.

Thirty minutes later, over coffee and laughter in a diner near home, we thanked God for a trucker and answered prayer.

"But next year," Scotty said, helping me with my coat, "I'm finding out where that guy bought that incredible tackle box."

"*Next* year?" I whooped.

My husband grinned.

Speak When You're Angry, and . . .

We'd just finished watching a program during which we'd been entertained by cowboys, shoot-outs, and Indians. "Imagine how many dead bodies there'd have been if I'd packed a pistol in the Wild West!" I said, recalling how, earlier in the day, I'd hit the horn long and hard when some driver had nearly sideswiped me.

"Dead bodies?" my husband grinned. "Babe, I doubt anyone would feel really threatened." He laughed. "About all you've ever done is shoot yourself in the foot."

I once read, "Speak when you're angry, and you'll make the best speech you'll ever regret." The author was right. So was my spouse. More times than I wanted to remember, I had shot myself in my own foot—usually the one in my own mouth.

I grew up believing anger was clout, that an enraged adult was one to be taken seriously. True, confrontation didn't exactly suit my nature and was actually something I feared. Even as an adult, I preferred making excuses, refused to face folks head-on. I'd force a smile, hold my anger in. But holding anger in only made it *seem* to go away—until one of those proverbial straws. Then, I'd erupt, nearly send my victim reeling, sever yet another relationship—all because I didn't know how to be heard without exploding from the inside out. A while back, however, things came to a head, and I decided it was time I learned another way. Since the day I began to try, I can see how God's been helping me, though sometimes it felt like I'd been set up!

I'd been writing for just two years when I received my first book contract. I was ecstatic! I was also ill-prepared for the fear that surfaced—a fear that the contract had hidden within it "fine print." A man who'd been in the business longer than I insisted I flatly state I wouldn't sign "unless." So, I called the editor. She was gracious but firm. I made an idle threat. She suggested alternatives. I lost my composure *and* my book contract.

Then a friend called late one night. I was overtired, she was overworked. I understood why she was "imposing" on me, but instead of meeting her halfway, I whipped out reflexive, angry words. She responded in kind. I held my ground—and came away from the confrontation minus not just one but several friends.

A couple of months ago, I wrote my former friend and asked her forgiveness. She said she'd forgiven me long ago. Would I forgive her? We've patched up our relationship, yes, but wasted months, years.

Next, I blew it in a setting where they really don't need proof that Christianity doesn't work. I'd returned merchandise to a department store. The returns hadn't been credited. My account was showing a substantial late charge.

"Late?" I shrieked at the credit manager. "I'll *never* shop here again!" I ripped my card in two and walked out, muttering vows. And did any of this result in anything good? No, it did not. I've never received the credit, have no card, and worse, I fear showing my face around there again. It is written, "Do not be quickly provoked in your spirit, for anger resides in the lap of fools" (Eccles. 7:9). Only days after my split with the local department store, I saw that was definitely the truth.

My husband had been overcharged. But did he rant? rave? Did he insult everyone in the entire shopping mall? No, he did not. Instead, he calmly explained—and with laughter—that he understood how mix-ups can occur. For his patience, he received his credit, *and* today he walks into and out of that store with *his* conscience clear.

Sometimes it seems as if I've spent most of my life angry. But even Jesus expressed anger, didn't He? He did, but there's a dark side to anger too, and that's the side I'd come to know all too well. I'd suffered from chronic bronchitis, asthma, depression, and a stomach that constantly acted up. A doctor suggested it was anger. A friend pointed out it was time to take my temper to God.

Prayers became pleas. "Help me, show me better ways," I begged. What He showed me was His Word, showed me it was time I planted it in my heart. With His help and His Word, I *could* change.

Today I'd like to say I have total victory, but I don't. There are still times when I feel so angry. On occasion, I still write letters when I'm provoked. But today I don't seal the envelopes, don't apply stamps. I wait and, waiting, I rethink and pray for another plan. I'm learning how to make myself heard without shouting, retreating, *or* fighting back. I'm also learning a gentle answer *does* turn away wrath (Prov. 15:1). No more shoot-outs for me.

Last Call for an Honest No

"You know, some days I'm actually glad when my children are sick. Gives me a good excuse to say no."

"I feel the same way about three feet of snow," I said. "Keeps folks housebound, unable to get to me."

Both my friend and I had felt led to serve the Body. Phyllis worked in the Christian school. I wrote for Sunday School papers and Christian women's magazines. But some days there were too few hours and too many demands because we'd accepted and added "just one more" responsibility to our lists.

"Still, we *are* meeting people's needs. Right?" we

would tell each other and ourselves. And that's what I honestly thought until the evening my husband pointed out several flaws in my rationale.

First, because I almost never meant it when I said I wanted to become involved, I'd lied. Nothing about a lie could be called ministry. Second, though I felt I'd been called to write, wasn't I spending a great deal of my time doing just about everything else? Could I actually say I'd persevered? Wasn't perseverance singleness of purpose, constancy, steadiness? And, what about godliness, being devout, sincere? There was nothing honorable about saying an outloud yes while silently shrieking angry oaths!

On all points I'd failed. In most cases it was too late to make amends. It was not too late, however, to decide, "Not one more made-up excuse." From now on I'd be honest. I'd say it nicely, but I would, when necessary, say no.

Innocent Blood

I'd heard "jokes" about government employees before, but I hadn't expected to hear them at a Christian seminar.

"What is a paradox?" one conferee asked. "And could you give us an example of redundancy?"

"A paradox," the instructor said, "is like 'government workers.'"

Several laughed.

"And redundancy?"

"An example would be '*unnecessary* government workers.'"

Some laughed, but I did not. My husband works for the government.

Ten minutes later, the instructor was asked to recommend a book.

"I could recommend this one," she said, "if you're interested in writing personal experience articles. But I *could not* recommend the author as a person. I hear she's into witchcraft, the occult, that sort of thing."

My spine fused. I'd known this author. She was a Christian. She wrote for the secular press, but she'd also written for Christian publishers.

I wanted to demand that the speaker retract her charges. Instead I said nothing at all as I began to wonder: how often had I, without weighing my words, rattled off careless remarks about another? How often had I, lacking wisdom, falsely accused?

"These six things doth the Lord hate: yea, seven are an abomination unto him: . . . a false witness that speaketh lies, and he that soweth discord among brethren" (Prov. 6:16, 19, KJV).

Make Time for Musing

Goals listed on scraps of paper covered my refrigerator and bathroom mirror: sewing, baking, candy making. We were going home. I'd need someone to grab the mail and paper, feed the dog, water plants.

Our departure date circled in red, I allotted only one day for gift gathering, arrived at the stores too early, and pressed my nose against windows, waiting impatiently for doors to open up.

Finally, my list in my fist, I ran from counter to counter, stuffed bags, and one hour later, dashed outdoors for home. But now there were hundreds of cars, and they all looked alike!

Wandering between rows of vehicles, I peered over parcels, stammered a frenzied prayer, and spotted our sedan.

Leaning against a fender, I balanced boxes, fumbled for and hooked my keys, felt my way around the lock, and practically flew across town and onto our street.

Once home, I entered the house, returned for the packages, opened the passenger door, and shrieked! Someone had stolen the gifts! Not until I'd blinked tears and wished offenses on robbers did I realize I'd poked my head into the passenger window of my daughter's car—not mine.

Hoping no neighbor had caught my performance, I swaggered nonchalantly toward the house.

Once inside, however, I hopped, skipped, and jumped toward the spare room, hid packages, and headed again for my list.

Too busy for breakfast, my stomach now churned.

"Popcorn," I decided. I'd eat with my right hand, iron with my left. But, instead of popcorn, I grabbed the decaf canister, spooned eight scoops of Sanka into the popper, and hit the switch!

"Read your devotional." The prompting wasn't loud, but it was clear.

"Read December 24," I heard.

"But, today's not the 24th!" I argued. By now, however, I was thoroughly overwrought and becoming willing. So I rummaged through devotionals, located December 24, and received what I'd needed for days.

"We should be better Christians if we were more alone; we should do more if we attempted less and spent more time in retirement and quiet waiting upon God. Time so spent is not lost time."

I hadn't added "enjoy a quiet moment" to my lists in more than a week.

"O Lord," I whispered, calm at last, "grant me the good sense to make time for musing, that I might give my family the best Christmas yet—by resting in You. Amen."

Everyone Knows?

Some mornings our Sunday School class seems so at odds with itself, I wonder how its members ever ended up under one roof. We've such diverse ways of seeing and approaching God. We choose up sides and disagree aloud. And heaven help the individual who expresses a notion not held by any other member of the group!

Recently, I suggested it was possible non-Christians didn't know they were doing wrong.

"*Everyone* knows right from wrong!" a class member declared. "*Everyone* knows what we're not supposed to do!"

"Everyone?" I asked. "Could we then assume 'everyone' believes God exists? that the Bible is His Word?"

The class divided. Those who believed the "everyone knows" theory became adamant. Within minutes, those of us with questions withdrew.

On another Sunday, someone had spotted a middle-aged couple reading on their patio.

"Obviously, they weren't Christians," the informant said.

The more vocal members of the class agreed. Those of us who weren't so certain kept our thoughts to ourselves.

How quick crowds are to prescribe and to judge. How glad I am our Lord is not a member of a crowd—that He is slow to rebuke, quick to offer compassion, willing to touch the eyes of those who will, just as they are, approach Him.

Brand-new Because God . . .

We'd returned to our beginnings unprepared to face our pasts—areas where we'd failed, lived unholy lives, sinned. Away for more than a dozen years, we'd come to know Christ, had asked for and received forgiveness, experienced joy, love, growth, and change. Now, former acquaintances either ignored us, convinced us we hadn't changed at all, or watched to see if our new natures might slip up.

"I wish we'd never moved back," I said.

My husband agreed. It seemed improbable we'd convince people we were who we now wanted to be, people who both loved and trusted God.

Together we made a decision. We would quit trying to explain or look changed.

"*We* can't erase our pasts," we decided. We could only know that Christ could and did.

We are the least worthy, but our transformation is fact because *He* has given us new life. As we come to accept and walk in that truth, we are learning to live our best, wherever He plants us, brand-new.

The Master Switch

For nearly a year, I'd prayed several times a week with my neighbor, a new Christian from up the road. More than once, however, I'd come away from our minutes together both enthusiastic and disturbed.

I was enthusiastic when Janet eagerly expressed her

desire to know the Lord more completely, shared a scripture she was just beginning to understand, radiated because she'd received a clear and thrilling answer to prayer. I was disturbed when things did not go as my neighbor had hoped and she turned to *me* expecting some solution. I was disturbed because on too many occasions I'd disappointed her.

How, I wondered, can I be expected always to come up with explanations for my friend when I'm frequently feeling just as confused?—when I'm also wondering, "What do we do now?"

Then one day, while working at my home computer, my monitor's screen flashed and dimmed. The printer clanked off, then on. Overhead lights and table lamps flickered and clicked throughout the house. There were snapping noises and an odd scent and a feeling in the air that spelled, "Storm on the way!"

My husband had explained such an event was a possibility. "You'll have to respond quickly," he'd said, reminding me thunder and lightning in our part of the world had the ability to completely destroy my machines. He'd also sat down beside me, read the owner's manual aloud, noted each of the steps I was to follow if I wanted to save my data and my dearly purchased gadgets, contraptions, and tools.

By the third time my monitor blinked, however, I became so rattled I couldn't even think where I'd filed the instructions, let alone read! So, I did the only thing I could think of to do. I went straight for the switch that controls the whole works and shut it down. And when Janet called later that afternoon, I told her to do the same.

"We may not always know what, exactly, follows 'It is written,'" I said. "Some days, we may feel under attack, totally bewildered, and have no answer to our 'Why?' But one thing's certain; we both know who covers it all. So when you can't remember word for word what Scripture says, just call on the name of Jesus. Engage the Master Switch."

He Will *Never* Leave nor Forsake

In Heb. 13:5 how often have we read, "Never will I leave you; never will I forsake you," and thought, Oh, sure? We've walked through divorce, missed out on promotions, lost jobs. We've wondered where college tuition will come from for an eager, brilliant teen. We've crossed and re-crossed the floors at night with a desperately feverish child. We've been made widows, and suddenly we wonder if anything could have prepared us for this. And, though we try with every ounce of faith we can muster, we just can't quite swallow the "never" bit. We can't quite make ourselves believe God hasn't turned His head this time, forgotten, or worse, abandoned us. When the Christian women I know are candid, most admit they've been there. But recently, I discovered something in Scripture I've never seen before. I discovered the *literal* meaning of leave and forsake, the *intent* behind these words.

According to my concordance, in the original Greek, when the Lord said "leave" in this passage, He meant "to send up or back." When He said He would never "forsake," He meant "leave down in."

Several years ago my husband's work took him to Nigeria, and while there he observed something he loves to relate.

Come sundown, a group of Nigerian mothers would gather their babies and toddlers beside the river for baths.

Each mother would then take a child, soap it, and soap it again from head to toe, until each one was covered with suds. Securing a child's wrists in one hand, she'd dunk the youngster up and down, not once but several times. She would dunk each of her charges so that the river entirely covered his or her head. And then, with a vigorous snap she'd yank the child up into the air. After several dunkings and when all offspring had been thoroughly scrubbed and rinsed, the mother would put her strong arms around each laughing wiggler and wrap each child in a good-night hug.

Sometimes Christian women feel as if they've been yanked up and out of their comfort zones and that they're dangling midair. Sometimes they feel that God has jerked them around, submerged them completely, allowed the waters to swallow them up. On occasion, even women who know better may feel deserted, overwhelmed, deep in frigid waters. But God has promised: He will not send us up or back or down beyond His love or watchfulness. Like those Nigerian mothers, He has His children—you and me—secure within His powerful, gentle grip.

Praise Blossoms

The day was dismal. Rain—not the sort that cleans the air, but only a drizzle—filled the sky with gray clouds, dripped onto and through window screens, seeped into corners of the house, and thoroughly dampened my spirit.

I had just undergone a third oral surgery, and though I certainly wasn't bedridden, I was confined. That it was raining seemed unfair. Since early morning, I'd barely managed to talk myself into putting one foot in front of the other.

Selecting work I might easily handle—and still rest, as the doctor had prescribed—I'd occupied my study most of the day.

Eventually, several manuscripts were ready for the mail. I shuffled across the room, stooped to the postal scale, and spotted the blossoms.

I hadn't expected them. In fact, I hadn't anticipated a geranium would bloom at all before spring—and then only after it had been relocated on the sunporch again. But it had blossomed not just once, but twice! Cherry red petals against the navy blue paper transported me from the pits to a place where the sun sang.

Grateful for the plant's beauty, I lifted my eyes and exclaimed, "O Father. Thank You for these two wonderful blossoms. They're absolutely beautiful! Thank You, Father, for blessing me."

My spirits lifted. I returned to my work, stamped envelopes, and watched the clock, remembering my friend, Kathy, had said she might stop by.

Midafternoon the doorbell rang, and on my doorstep I discovered not only my friend but also a plant covered with no less than 200 miniature blossoms in what else but bright, cherry red!

"Here," she offered, laughing, "these are from the Lord!"

My mouth dropped open, and before I could close it and gather my wits, Kathy continued.

"I thought it was a little early to come by, so I decided to pass the time browsing through that nursery at the crossroads. I haven't been in there before."

She smiled as she shut the door behind her with one hand and with the other held the plant out toward me. "Every single time I walked by this thing, the Lord kept

34

bringing *you* to mind. It was as if He kept saying, 'Nancy. Nancy.' Pretty soon I got it: He wanted it delivered to *you.* So here you are! For whatever reason, the flowers are from Him."

At first I was unable to respond. I simply stood there speechless and staring.

We visited for nearly an hour, my mind wandering as red petals caught my eye. Each time I glanced in their direction, I realized it was still raining; but, for me, it didn't matter anymore. I'd been reminded of something I'd heard our pastor say, something I'd considered "just words" at the time. But now it made sense. Now I could understand. "If we sow praises for small beginnings," our pastor had said, "the Lord will give the increase—a hundredfold."

And He did.

When Christians Become One

Because of my husband's work, we are frequently moved. As soon as we've settled in, we begin to look for our church home. But this experience hasn't always been good. Why? Because of what Christians have had to say to us about steering clear of one congregation or another and who isn't exactly "lined up."

Yes, on occasion, the warnings were well-founded. Too often, however, they've seemed based on prejudice, lack of knowledge, jealousy, fear. When we've ignored such advice, we've often found just what we were looking for and needing—a place in which to worship God, a church in which the Word was taught without compromise.

When there is such dissension within the Body and

division and strife between denominations and fellowships, how can we expect a disbelieving world to accept and embrace Christ?

What could they possibly see about Him in us?

Are We Simple—Those of Us Who Believe?

We hadn't seen him in years, but when we heard his voice on the phone, we sensed nothing about his life was the same. We weren't prepared, however, for tattered clothing and the way his shoulders dipped.

At the table he fumbled for words, spilled dinner on his lap, dropped names we'd only read about in books, mentioned million-dollar homes, big cars, gourmet food, and drink. With no time for religion or his mother's God, he'd "run with the best."

But his wife had left him. He had no children and no one else. His career was over and all that he'd held dear. And tonight, in ragged sweater and shoes, he seemed simple and poor.

How often I'd envied such well-known people with more money than only enough. But tonight, as we promised home-cooked meals again soon, this man fought tears—and I returned to my warm, plain kitchen and a hug from my godly, unpretending spouse.

Coming Clean

My husband had begun traveling three weeks out of four. We'd prayed for a job change, a move home to Montana, where the pace would be slow and our time would belong to us. But the answer had been no.

To add to my frustration, East Coast weather hadn't been exactly wonderful. Fifteen degrees below the springtime norm. Crabgrass had taken over. So had dandelions, grubs, and moles.

Now, after what seemed just too much rain and too much time alone, I wanted conversation, comforting. I'd been living on popcorn and salad bars, clipping grocery-store coupons, looking forward to cooking for and talking to someone other than myself.

Scotty, on the other hand, had been in a week's worth of meetings, arbitrating, trying to make first one and then another overbooked flight. *He* wanted to be left alone.

I don't remember which last straw did it, but I do remember bounding down the cellar stairs, jaws clenched, and seizing an oversized comforter—one I'd stuffed into a trunk months earlier because it didn't fit into my washing machine and would have to be scrubbed at a Laundromat. This would be my excuse to run away from home. If Scotty wouldn't listen, I'd retreat to magazines and candy bars and watch my wash spin around.

A washer loaded and full of soap, I seated myself on a hard, wobbling chair. I tried concentrating on what wasn't exactly shaping up to be reading material, flipped pages forward, then back. I couldn't quit thinking about my "inconsiderate" spouse. The man hadn't listened to one single word I'd said.

Yes, I understood these separations made life difficult

for him too. But that didn't negate the fact that he'd been insensitive.

"Men! They're all alike," I murmured behind my magazine—and spotted a woman who'd waited on me at a discount store. Weary, worn, old before her time, she was loading not one washer, but eight.

While I watched, she trudged to the change machine and those runty boxes of soap, returned to claim a string of washers in a row, shoved coins into metal cartridges, dumped powders, slammed lids, and drew on a cigarette she'd lit the minute she'd slapped her plastic baskets down onto the concrete floor.

She works all day, every day, I recalled. Now she spends her free time doing eight loads of wash?

At our house, we were hard-pressed to come up with more than two. Much of what my husband wore he took to the cleaners on his days off so I "wouldn't have to wrestle with it."

I pictured Scotty with his arms full of jackets and slacks—grinning, asking if I wanted to ride along—proposing breakfast or coffee on the way back home.

But, this morning, he has made me so mad . . .

I'd no sooner set my face like a flint when the other woman's husband entered the rattling, clammy room, shoulders slouched, bill cap on tilt, denims dangling from nearly invisible hips, and a brown cigarette hanging from one corner of his mouth. A pout cut across his narrow face.

He hadn't said one word to his wife when two teenage girls bounded through double doors and joined the pair.

Oh, good, I thought, they're all going to help. But they weren't. The girls wanted change for a Coke machine. The man wanted his wife's undivided attention.

Giggling, the daughters departed, while the man leaned against a washer to coach his wife.

Maybe he's just waiting until he's done with his cigarette. Then he'll give her a hand, I decided. I recalled how Scotty often thoughtfully helped me.

Again I focused on the husband and wife who weren't yet functioning as a team. The man was lighting up again while his wife literally ran from washers to dryers and back.

"Help her!" I wanted to shout. "Scotty would!"

"You gonna be done here pretty soon?" the sullen man asked, as if he had other plans and his wife was holding him back.

She nodded, drew smoke deep into the shell of her, and dragged her frame on ragged shoes to a coin machine.

For the next half hour, the woman worked and the man watched. The daughters exited and reentered at predictable intervals to announce they needed more money and wished their mother would "hurry up!"

I don't believe this! If I had all that wash, Scotty would never expect me to manage alone. The nights he was home, didn't he always dry dishes for me? And what about mornings? While I cooked breakfast and packed his lunch, didn't he usually make the bed? When he needed a shirt, didn't he often iron it himself? Had he once complained?

The surly man's disagreeable voice interrupted my telling myself the truth.

"Maybe I'll go see what the kids are up to," he said.

"Go see what the kids are up to?" I wanted to shout. "Help your wife!" I stood straight up out of my chair. "Scotty would," I said aloud—and Scotty walked through the door.

He was still wearing the faded shoes he'd donned to dig in his garden because "Gardens can't wait!" He wore the long-sleeved, weathered shirt he'd "captured" from my Salvation Army bag, because he planned to chop poison ivy out of our hedge. "Won't just disappear by itself!" he'd snapped.

"Scotty! Why are *you* here?" I blurted, noting how that even when he was agitated, his blue eyes gave his tenderness away.

"Babe," he said, his voice husky, "I haven't been very good to you." He cleared his throat, stuffed his hands into the pockets of his jeans—looking like the cowboy he'd been when we married.

I wanted to fling my arms around my husband's neck. I felt like a heroine in a paperback romance.

"I'm taking you to lunch," he said. "*You* are much more important than any garden," he added. "Besides, it gets lonely at home . . . when you're not there."

I wouldn't cry and I wouldn't kiss my husband in a Laundromat. But I'm sorely tempted, I thought to myself.

"Your comforter done?" Scotty asked.

I'd forgotten I owned a comforter, let alone that it was taking up badly needed space. "Yes," I nodded, "I just have to fold it and then . . ."

He'd turned his back to me. He wasn't listening. He's leaving, I thought.

"Come on, Babe," he said, smiling over his shoulder. "I'll give you a hand," he added, at the dryer door now, pulling yards of pink tulips and green leaves out onto the folding table across the room.

I glanced at the woman whose wash was nearly dry. She'd be folding forever. I glowered at her spouse who was jingling coins and mumbling something about "going for ice cream with the girls." And I touched Scotty's face where his laugh lines show, no longer caring what strangers thought.

Kissing my husband's cheek, I told him I was sorry, that I loved him, that I was grateful for the marriage we shared.

The folding finished, I admitted I had been having

more than a little difficulty with the frequent separations and strained weekends—weekends when we felt as if we were just getting to know one another again.

"Me too, Babe," Scotty said, his palm warm and comforting at the nape of my neck.

I turned sideways to catch one last glimpse of the man glaring at his watch and rapping his boot at his wife.

I tucked my fingers into Scotty's as we headed for the door and lunch. "I'm still glad you're my husband," I whispered, just below my spouse's ear, "even if you do travel."

He squeezed my hand.

"Because," I said, "truth is, you're very good to me."

One Day . . .

We'd purchased our first brand-new home and, to cut costs, we'd decided to do the landscaping ourselves. We agreed we'd moved to Montana for the fishing, the outdoors, to relax. But the lawn couldn't wait, could it? Weren't neighbors already plotting beds and seeding even before they'd moved in? We couldn't float the Yellowstone while our acre-plus went to stubble and hay. We'd get our place in order—*then* we'd play. We could put in a couple of trees, shrubs, and start some grass. There'd still be plenty of summer for fun.

A local supermarket had advertised bedding plants. I'd scatter just a few around the patio for color and some near the front door and a few pots on the deck. Wouldn't take all that long.

Meanwhile, summer grew warm; the sky, blue and magnificent. Scotty and I began heading outdoors about the time the meadowlarks and white-tailed deer showed up. We'd rake and imagine croquet. A landscaper picked rocks for us, but we were left with dirt that needed weeding, and *someone* had to level the ground. So, we leveled. At the nursery, they showed us how to place beds, read a blueprint, arrange plants artfully. Then, the industrial-strength edging arrived.

The black, rubber edging took more than the one day we'd expected. It took us an entire week. But things were shaping up. Yes, occasionally we heard fishing was good, but right now we needed to save ourselves some money by hauling all the plants ourselves. We gathered rope, canvas, boxes, and tarp—for what would become the first of more than one dozen trips from north of town to south.

Trees and shrubs were not planted quickly. We discovered we could just about wear ourselves out digging holes, cutting twine and burlap wrap. There was the matter of spacing and food to be sprinkled into every hole, trees to stake because wind can be fatal. The flowers wanted special care.

Meanwhile, friends called. They were going fishing. Backpacking trips had been planned. Could we come for barbecue?

"Thanks, sounds wonderful." But we'd take a rain check when our 150 plants were in place and the garage was in order and windows were clean again. These *weren't* excuses. We'd made a mess in the garage, the windows had been dealt with by the new sprinkler system, and we'd stirred up a lot of dust. We couldn't be paddling an inner tube down the river with our windows so filthy that folks couldn't see in or out! But we'd get it together—one day.

"One day" finally came toward the latter part of August. Backs aching, tempers on edge, hands blistered, and years older, we surveyed our landscaped home with pride—and the very next day the weather changed—*dras-*

tically. Fishing wasn't so good, they said. Our place looked terrific, but summer had come and gone.

Have I learned anything? I ask myself. Haven't there been other summers, other happy plans, other precious moments missed because I've worked when I might have played, and later regretted it?

Summer's beginning to bloom again. This year we've been told the lawn should be fed, and we won't want the weeds to get away from us. All the beds are crying for color. The windows are dirty again, the garage is still a mess. But will we tie our time to chores or allow ourselves to sit, play, do nothing at all?

We won't want the weeds to get away from us. What about quiet times, our children's times, hours spent together with books or fishing rods under a summer sun?

"Don't forget my waders!" I whoop to my grinning husband as he loads the truck. And I remind myself, donning my lucky hat, the lilies of the field never toil, and even sparrows have homes. Yes, it's true weeds happen, but waste God's summer gifts? Allow the pleasure of playing to get away from us?

Not me, not today.

Get Carried Away! Rejoice!

"You don't have to get carried away," a fellow worshiper had said. But I was praising the God who'd done wonderful things in my life! I was no longer ill, depressed, bound by childhood memories. He had delivered me. I'd tried silence and rejoicing privately, but I couldn't seem to do it—until after the censure, that is.

Back home, however, my joy would not be contained. I'd leap to my feet in the middle of my work and shout, "Thank You, Lord!" I did wonder sometimes, though, just exactly how *He* felt about *me*. Then, one morning when I'd been particularly demonstrative, the thought came to me that even God might think I was a little bit weird. When I clapped, did He think I was ridiculous? When I cheered, did He think I should keep still? "Yes, Lord," I said, "I wonder—I do." I was in the middle of wondering when the phone rang.

"Nancy?" It was a friend from church. "The oddest thing just happened," she said, laughter in her voice. "I could be mistaken, but I don't think so," she added, sounding as if she were taking a deep, deep breath.

"Mistaken?" I asked. "About what?"

"Well, I'd just decided to sit down for my quiet time when the Lord seemed to be telling me to call you." She laughed again.

The Lord wanted her to call me? "Why? I don't understand. You're kidding."

"He wants you to know something," she said, taking another deep breath. "He delights in you!"

"When he came near the place . . . the whole crowd of disciples began joyfully to praise God in loud voices for all the miracles they had seen" (Luke 19:37).

How could they not?

Just Walking in Love

With my youngest in school, I planned to ship cookware to my eldest, dash to the copy shop, deposit film, and stand in line at the post office again. My husband had the "good" car. I'd drive the one with shredding seats, oil leaks, and a slipping clutch. Many thoughts crossed my mind—prayer and gratitude never did.

The shipping clerk hadn't returned from lunch. There were at least a dozen customers waiting: agitated women, fidgeting kids, a barking dog, a cigar-puffing man, and me—every single one of us locked outside in humidity so high we nearly dropped. But, just about the time I'd decided I was going home, a young man with cleated boots kicked open the door and *ordered* us inside.

He hadn't yet turned on the lights, but he was roaring, "Next!" He also roared at two preschoolers who were twirling and dancing around their mom.

"Fill out your slips!" he barked at the others as he grabbed the box I'd so carefully packed.

"I don't have a slip," I said, half afraid, half mad. "Father," I thought, as I gave up my place in line, "This isn't going so well." I backed up, apologized, wrestled my packages to the floor and, with one foot, pushed them across the concrete.

By the time I'd filled out the correct slip, the line had stretched. The mother (whose children were now singing) stepped forward. Without so much as a warning, the clerk raised a fist, slammed it onto the counter, and thundered that he wanted "those kids" quiet, and he wanted them quiet now! The mother burst into tears, the rest of us stared at the floor, and the tyrant ordered me to "lift 'em onto the scale."

I'd hoped for help, but he offered none. Instead, he tapped his pencil while I pushed, pulled, and heaved both cartons onto the counter that, for me, was nearly chest-high.

He barked the weight and what it was I owed him. It was more than I'd anticipated. I tried to explain I didn't have enough and that I'd forgotten to bring my checkbook. But my packages marked "Fragile" were dumped, and the next customer was told to step forward or get out of the way.

Slamming my trunk lid, I was ready for tears, a tantrum, and home. But the list on my dashboard read, "Drugstore." So that's where I went, only to discover after I'd driven around the block half-a-dozen times looking for a place to park, that they were out of what I'd come for. The salesgirl was hot and tired, a dog had gotten loose, two boys were racing up and down aisles trying to catch it—and the manager was glaring at *me!* He thought *I* was the mother of the boys *and* the dog.

I spun on one heel, glowered, and headed for the next stop on my list.

The woman at the photo counter was taking a cigarette break. I fished for envelopes, mentioned my car was parked in a fire zone, and received not the ballpoint pen I'd requested but a glassy-eyed stare. I stared back.

Eventually, the clerk waited on me—before someone from the fire department showed up—and I slammed the key into the ignition wondering, What am I doing wrong?

I'd already settled into the driver's seat when I discovered I was blocked in. "Lord . . . ," I moaned, "I have had it. I don't care if those packages ever get shipped. I'll never go back into that drugstore again. They can keep those idiot prints! And if that woman who's fenced me in doesn't move, I'm going to back right into her brand-new car and give *her* something to be angry about!"

By now I knew for certain I bore *no* resemblance to the "virtuous woman," but I was too mad to care.

Within minutes, the other driver frowned at me in her side-view mirror and coasted forward as I peeled out of that lot like someone who'd just robbed the mall.

Are you going to be defeated again? The thought came very close to being audible.

"Lord . . . ," I wailed, "I can't stand it! That poor mother and that obnoxious clerk. I won't go back even when I *do* get cash. I haven't picked up half of what was on my shopping list. And what about those pictures I'm supposed to have by tomorrow? I don't ever want to deal with that woman again."

I was immediately reminded of notes on my bulletin board: "Persevere regardless!" and "Praise the Lord anyhow!"

OK, so I would follow my list, go to the copier's—the place I dreaded most. Machines and I don't get along. I despised going into that place. I usually ended up with black borders around everything or copies so light they couldn't be read.

Shoving swinging doors, I moaned. Every single machine was tied up, and the clerk who sometimes helped was on the phone. I couldn't wait; I had to pick my daughter up from school. This was the last straw. I was going on home, and I would not run errands, and . . .

"Hi! You need copies made?" The voice behind me sounded like a song.

I turned and discovered a round, brown-eyed, smiling face. "I do. But the machines are taken," I said, shrugging.

"Oh, I'll get 'em for you." She smiled, took my papers, and as we crossed the carpet to a copier hidden behind plants, I couldn't help but notice the bounce in the smiler's step.

"This new?" I asked.

"Sure is." The girl seemed not to notice the edge to my voice. "Brand-new!" she said, her lilt lessening the tightness in my neck.

"Well, you'll have to show me how to run it," I said. "Machines and I don't get along." I smiled; it felt good.

The girl laughed. "Well, this one's easy," she said, and my shoulders began to relax.

47

"Well, that's good," I said. "But may I just see one copy before you do 'em all? If they don't look good, I might not get paid."

"Oh? What do you do?" She looked at me with genuine interest—no cigarette, no barking, no glassy stare.

Instantly, I wished I hadn't mentioned . . . "I write," I said. I cleared my throat.

"You do?" Again she glowed. "What do you write?"

"Well . . . articles." Why couldn't I have just kept still? "For Christian magazines mostly," I said.

She nearly leaped up off the floor. "You're a Christian?" she asked, her eyes wide open now.

It's no wonder she has to ask, I thought. I nodded a yes.

She threw her arms upward. "Well, hallelujah!" she said, her volume turned up.

I noted several eavesdroppers, but I didn't care. Something good was happening. I wasn't about to back up and leave this time. Instead, I shared and we laughed, and she talked about Jesus all the way from presenting me with clean copies to the cash register. By the time I'd paid her, I'd also confessed—told her how defeated and angry I'd felt and how I'd acted. I hadn't behaved like much of a Christian, I said.

She smiled. "Well, Honey, when I come up against people and situations that ruffle me wrong, I just walk in love toward 'em." Her eyes twinkled as she smiled her beautiful smile. "And you know what? I just don't have to let them make me feel bad!"

Her joy was contagious. More than one person on my side of the counter was listening now.

She counted my change and patted my arm. "Just walk in love," she crooned, as I backed toward the exit and slipped through swinging doors.

Within minutes, I was given two opportunities to test

my new friend's theory, and it worked. It worked at the crowded milk store *and* at the gas station, where there were more customers than pumps. And as I drove toward home, smiling and praising again, I knew it was true: the choice was mine. I could give up or get mad *or* walk in love.

A Loner—but Always Happy Alone?

On a scale of 0 to 100 (with 0 representing the most extroverted and 100 those who wish to be entirely alone), I recently scored 74. Introvert. So, when my husband was sent to the Middle East and our daughter returned to a college 3,000 miles from home, I said, "No problem. I need no one to fill *my* hours. I'm a loner. Right?" Besides, I had my work. I'd be busy, content. That's what I thought until the day *after* my husband flew out.

Scotty departed Philadelphia on a Friday. Saturday morning, the house felt empty and cold. OK, I'd listen to TV. "It'll seem like someone's here with me." But the television hadn't been running 20 minutes when it spluttered, flickered, and quit.

"Well, who cares?" I said aloud. "I hadn't actually planned to watch it anyway. I can always bring the old black and white up from the basement. I'll be fine."

Later that morning, however, while working at my computer, I began to feel lonely again. Maybe I would call my nearest neighbor, a widow. She might enjoy lunch out. But when I put my ear to the receiver, I discovered the line was dead.

The television was one thing, but the phone too?

About now I wondered if my husband would ever come home. How long had he been gone? I looked at the calendar, then at the clock on the kitchen wall—12 hours so far. Just 7 weeks, 6 days, and 11 hours to go.

I ran down our drive and across the road, borrowed the phone, said I had hoped to meet her for lunch, but it wasn't going to work out. I told her I was sorry, then hurried back home.

Three hours later the repairman arrived, but he wouldn't come in.

"If I do," he said, "it'll cost you big bucks."

My wheels spun. My husband had left me the checkbook, of course, and I certainly knew all about budgets and managing money on my own. But what sort of "big bucks" was he talking about? So big I'd be cut off from the world beyond my home?

"You've got to come in. My husband's out of the country and I'm alone, and I *can't* be without a phone!"

"Nope," he said. "Checked the lines, nothin' wrong."

"Yes, there *is*," I said. "My phone's dead, kaput."

"Do what I say and you'll see," he said, pushing his bill cap from his forehead and wiping his brow with the back of his hand.

Within seconds, I discovered he was right; it was a jack in the back bedroom. "Jiggling" and "fiddling" restored our service just as the man promised it would.

Once again I decided, "No problem." I'd be fine. No, I couldn't go out with my neighbor now; it was too late for lunch, and she had evening plans. But tomorrow after church I'd treat myself to a ride in the country, visit glass and pottery outlets, enjoy driving around the Amish farms.

Sunday I followed through on my promise, and the drive out was wonderful. But during the return trip home, the car began making noises like nothing I'd ever heard. It wouldn't shift; I drove home in second gear.

"The clutch," the service station owner said. "Leave 'er sit till your hubby comes home."

"I won't survive without a car for that long!"

"Well, I'm not touching it," he said. "It's a hunk of junk. It might be he'll just say, 'Dump it.'"

Back home, I crawled into bed. "Scotty's only been gone two days, and *everything's* going wrong." But, determined I would not give in to despair, I added, "I'll *make* myself make it, even without a car."

However, come day three, I knew I'd been fooling myself. I couldn't yet admit I needed people, but I did concede I needed to get out of the house.

Where we were living, however, getting out was not so easy. No buses, sidewalks, shopping malls. Without a car, I could go nowhere.

"Lord, help!" I wailed—and within minutes the first answer to my prayer arrived on my doorstep in the form of a wife whose husband carpooled with mine.

"I was on my way for groceries and suddenly, in the middle of Paoli Pike, I remembered you're alone. Want to come along?"

In about 30 seconds flat, I'd gathered my purse, my shoes, and my coat.

On Tuesday a woman from the church called. "Say, I hear your husband's away. Why don't you visit our Bible study tomorrow?"

Bible study? I hadn't wanted to become involved. I had my work. I couldn't be gallivanting. "I have no car," I said.

"No problem; I'll come and get you."

"But I don't want you to drive all the way out here, week after week."

"If I find it doesn't work out for me, I'll just call one of the other girls," she said. "They won't mind."

Pride couldn't stop me; I said yes. And the following morning, I met with the women in the church.

Now I had something to look forward to Wednesdays, but what about the other six days of the week?

The answer came from a woman I'd spent a great deal of time avoiding.

"I know you want to join the aerobics class," she said, "so, I'm driving you, and I don't want any arguments." She'd wait for me in the church library; she had reading to do. So two days a week, I could look forward to the arrival of my new friend's car.

Time was beginning to pass. I had the Bible study and my exercise class. A couple began coming by on Saturday mornings, offering breakfast at McDonald's and a ride to the flea market for bargains and Amish goods.

Almost daily, one woman or another suggested outlet shopping or a run for books and tapes. Order was coming out of chaos. It seemed nothing else would go wrong and I'd manage just fine—until the night I caught the late night news. America had bombed Libya, and according to the globe in our den, my husband was much too close.

"Lord," I cried, terrified. Again, people reached out.

First, Scotty's secretary called to encourage. Men I'd never met—men who'd worked with my husband both in the States and abroad—reassured. Operators patiently worked through red tape. And though it took hours, I was—via transatlantic cables—united with my spouse.

While our voices and static threatened a disconnect, we prayed and I knew we would be OK.

The following morning, women called with invitations to lunch and dinner in their homes, picked me up when I had shopping to do, took me to coffee, prayed, and made certain I never missed church. And when my spouse returned, I went back to my writing room and thought, I'll be just as happy alone.

But the following week, I rejoined the Bible study, and two weeks later I met a friend for lunch. I even found myself making a promise to go shopping and knowing I would actually enjoy myself.

Yes, I'm a person most often content to be alone. Because of my nature and the nature of my work, it's necessary that I frequently withdraw. But those two months, with my husband away, I learned something I hadn't known before: I may feel I need space, and I may feel I need quiet—but I need people too.

Who Is My Neighbor?

I remember one winter we were living on the East Coast. Seemed that year all it did was snow, which was the last thing we needed in a distant, unfriendly metropolitan area. Icicles dangled from our bird feeder, fashioning a bulwark that turned all but the determined chickadees out.

Snow reeled and pitched, and the man next door plowed his drive. Not ours, not the new family's (the folks who'd recently moved into our neighborhood from the South and who didn't yet own a snowblower, let alone a plow), and not the widow's drive across the road.

Earlier that same winter my husband's work had taken him to the Southwest when we were caught off guard by the most overwhelming snowfall of the year. Scotty hadn't been out of sight 24 hours when it hit. It took me three days to dig a path to the main road. It took the widow three days too. Daily she'd shovel and sweep, then head for the house to rest. Come back out, try again. And the owner of the John Deere plow? He cleared one drive, his own.

Today I consider the cost of oil and gasoline. Maybe our former neighbor wasn't in a position to purchase fuel enough to plow three more drives. Maybe it never occurred to him we'd be happy to pay. Then, too, I suspect it's practically impossible to stay warm for long on an iced-up tractor seat. Besides, the man worked in the city and commuted an hour or more. Maybe he was too tired to clear more than one drive. Somehow, though, all my wondering doesn't make me feel much better about a man who could watch a widow shovel snow.

Today, with cities growing crowded and felt distance between people who were once friends, we don't seem to care much about the others anymore. We fence our spaces, attach answering machines to telephones—and not only in brooding city tracts. Out where the living is mostly rural I'm also beginning to notice that folks have little time for goodwill. Just the other day our closest neighbor ran his snowblower up and down his driveway and never once asked if I needed help, since my husband was away again. Even out and beyond the city I fear we're becoming cold.

I remember, in my childhood, visiting a cousin's wheat farm in eastern Washington. What fun to sojourn to where listening in on party lines (and proffering bits of advice) was the customary thing to do. Where people not only "talked a good game" but rolled up their sleeves because a neighbor needed help getting his crop in before the rains arrived. Where, when holsteins calved, fellow ranchers called. Where, Sundays, hired hands and family gathered around chicken-dinner tables that welcomed strangers as well.

I don't want to be too hard on the Eastern urbanite.

In our former neighborhood it took me three months to welcome a new family, to see if they needed anything.

Before he died, the husband of the widow used to say, "If you want a good neighbor, you have to be a good neighbor." And, this morning, I ask myself if I'm good. To tell you the truth, I don't remember when I did anything out of the ordinary or special for anyone who lives nearby, unless you want to count the time I took in the widow's mail when she went south. No, I don't think I can actually call that "special." I did feed her cat a couple of times. Didn't exactly put myself out, though.

My thesaurus suggests a lot of synonyms for the word "Neighbor." Words like "person next door" and "nearby dweller" and "fellow citizen." It also suggests "friend." And I remember a woman who recently wrote to tell me she's lived in her neighborhood for 13 years but doesn't know a single soul there. Another said she knew her neighbors but that, several years ago, there was some sort of a feud, and they'd all quit speaking to one another. They had even warned their children, "Say nothin' to no one and come straight home."

Neighborhoods? Not according to Webster. My dictionary says a neighbor is "one who lives on friendly terms with another."

I'm worried. It isn't just the snow and sleet and icicles six inches long. We humans have also begun to freeze up. I'm worried because my "we" includes me.

This morning I received a call from a woman who used to live next door. I remember my friend as determined, chirping, agreeable, and seeming never to be discontent. But next week she's moving to another state because she no longer feels she can cope. Her husband decided he doesn't care to be married anymore. Her child died several months ago. And no one from the neighborhood came—not to say they were sorry, nor to offer a shoulder to cry on or a cup of coffee in a breakfast nook.

This morning, with my former neighbor on the other end of the line, I wonder: if we don't turn ourselves around, are we going to build bulwarks so forbidding we'll shut even the chickadees out?

WINTER WHEAT

In the shadow of his hand hath he hid me, and made me a polished shaft.

ISA. 49:2, KJV

All Eyes on God

Her husband had been unemployed for over a year. She'd found temporary work. But so far, her spouse had been rejected by every local employer. Meanwhile, well-meaning advisers bombarded her with, "You shouldn't be working. It's your *husband's* place to provide for you. Leave him . . . he needs to wake up. God's withholding employment because you're in error in some area of your lives. The Lord's teaching you to get by with less. He wants you to become more aggressive. He wants you to rest. Start claiming a job—a high-paying one!"

"After a while, I didn't know who to believe," she said. "Seemed everyone had a different opinion. Morale at our house was deteriorating, and I was more weary and discouraged than I'd ever been before—until one morning during my quiet time."

My friend had just finished praying when she suddenly recalled God's promise—a promise to renew our strength. "I simply had to focus on Him," she said. "He's the One who created all things, including my spouse and myself. It was time to stop running to the others. It was time to turn to Him only, and to wait for Him to act. I could trust Him to keep us from falling; I would 'walk, and not faint'" (Isa. 40:31, KJV).

And she did.

"Father, thank You for supplying all of our needs—even strength. And, when we sometimes forget that You are ever mindful of us and the desires of our hearts, help us remember You have created all things. Help us remember so that we might not grow weary, that we might not faint. In Jesus' name. Amen."

Detours

In driving rain, we'd become completely turned around and disoriented in downtown Philadelphia. We'd checked maps and determined which avenues pointed toward home; but our guides made no mention of detours.

Though we noted each road sign and attempted to stay on course, we soon met a dead end. There was nothing we could do but back up, turn around, and try again.

Eventually, as we kept our eyes on the skyline and noted street names on posts above us, we advanced through the maze and rolled out onto the turnpike.

Relaxed at last, I considered how our Christian walks, though we try to press forward, are often blocked or temporarily confused. We make plans to persevere in a particular direction—heeding God's Word and sensing His unique plan for our individual routes through this life. But occasionally we become distracted by the world's persistent diversions—nudges to watch television for hours, sleep late, dillydally at shopping centers, or accept so-called free workouts at a local spa.

Though I've heard God call me to serve Him and I attempt to travel the route it appears He's laid out for me, too often I waste time on mortal entanglements—until I look up.

From time to time I've become confused, but when I turn for help, set my sights on Him, He keeps me on course so that I might continue to move forward and "attend upon the Lord without distraction" (1 Cor. 7:35, KJV).

I'm thankful that in life's detours His Word turns me around—that I might go on.

Press On

Overloaded and angry, I'd prayed, but I couldn't sit long enough for the sort of prayer my distress required. I couldn't get quiet, couldn't close my eyes, relax. So I decided to jog instead.

"Lord," was all I could manage as I measured my steps. "Help," I mumbled, rounding the bend where two horses grazed.

Yes, my husband had prayed, and my friend, Ann, had promised to do the same. But I longed for *His* reassurance, longed to see an end to the roadblocks, the depression, whatever it was that kept dealing with me.

Entering the woods, I tried to pray, but the words wouldn't come. Nearing a stream that wanders through low, bushy pine, I made mental lists of all I wanted to accomplish, wondered why it was that, for weeks, I'd accomplished little, succumbed to despair. Would I never be well again?

"Father . . . ," I exhaled, working to catch my breath, "help me to see what torments me, so that I'm of little use to my family, myself, You." And, at that very spot—where trees tower and the road seems to disappear in the shade—I heard above me a call sudden and clear.

"Fears, fears, fears, fears, worry, worry, worry, worry," the mockingbird sang. I had my answer. I knew what had kept me from seeing myself in His care. Worry. The enemy of faith. It was time to be done with it, time to trust, to press on.

Waiting on God

"Praise God! He's giving you the gift of waiting," my friend wrote. Obviously, she didn't understand. I hadn't written in nearly a year. When a writer's not writing . . . well, I'd told both my husband and my closest friends . . . I felt as if I might as well be dead. "I'm never going to get well," I said. I couldn't make myself write. I'd reached out to friends through letters. I'd confessed depression, admitted I seemed to have no say-so about what I would do with a day, declared my worst fear had come to pass: God had taken my work away for some sin I couldn't recall.

Soon, answers to my letters began to arrive. Several friends said they'd pray. Others suggested I plant myself before my computer and stare at the screen or at blank pieces of paper if I had to. But, then, an editor friend called. "Why don't you just 'be' for a while?" she suggested. "Do nothing. Just be."

"I don't know how!" I wailed. Still, if I couldn't force myself to work, I would have to find something to do with my time. So, I began to accept invitations to coffee, lunch, auctions, bazaars. Mornings, I took long walks and discovered I like it—the walking, meeting my neighborhood.

I began making quilts, stuffed animals, and dolls. My first grandchild was expected; I had shopping to do.

Today, what am I doing with my life? I'm being . . . and I'm waiting. I'm trusting and finally believing God *is* acquainted with all of my ways, even my lying down.

"You discern my going out and my lying down; you are familiar with all my ways" (Ps. 139:3).

Prisoner of Hope

"Return to your fortress, O prisoners of hope; even now I announce that I will restore twice as much to you" (Zech. 9:12).

Scotty had finally been told what we'd already begun to fear: he wouldn't be given the promotion he'd applied for, though he was more than qualified, though he'd been told earlier it would undoubtedly be his. That same week, I received 13 rejections in one batch of mail. Each of our disappointments seemed cruel—until a wonderful Christian friend called to say her daughter had died. We'd prayed and believed for her healing, but healing had not come.

How could my friend stand it? What in the world was she going to do? It was asking too much. Where was God?

Not one week later, my friend and I met for coffee *and* praise. Why praise? Not because we believe my husband's work situation will soon change. Not because we imagine my rejections will become acceptances after all. And, surely not because we believe my friend's daughter will walk back into her mother's life. We praised because He who has called us is faithful. He hasn't missed any of this. He loves us beyond what we can imagine or think. And, in due time, He will restore, make all things new.

In the past, I've believed that if only I could just talk directly to the publisher, invite my husband's superiors to our home . . . But seeing my husband walk through his disappointment and hearing my friend overcome her pain, I know that I have heard the Lord—heard Him say, "Hand over your concerns, your desires. Trust *Me*."

We're all tempted, I think, to fight our own battles, to wonder why *He* hasn't done something about what's going on. But He hasn't forgotten us. Within each of us He has planted a measure of faith, a whisper to "wait."

Yes, we are His prisoners—and He, because He loves us, is our Hope.

Wisdom or Foolishness?

"If only for this life we have hope in Christ, we are to be pitied more than all men" (1 Cor. 15:19). I read and I think of my friend Betty, who died of leukemia believing she would see Christ. I recall reading of martyrs who wouldn't deny Him. A friendship ends because a woman says, "No, I can't participate." A child wanders into a swamp and drowns, and her parents' faith remains strong. A friend's spouse abandons her to move in with a younger woman, and the abandoned wife continues to trust God.

Each of my friends believes in Christ. Each trusts that, although this life has been hard, the Lord will do as He has said. Each anticipates that, one day, they will see the home He has prepared for them.

Foolish? Yes, according to the world's view. But, looking at this life through faith, all that we read in God's Word is fact, right? *Not* believing would be the foolishness.

Search Me, O God

"Search me, O God, and know my heart; test me and know my anxious thoughts. See if there is any offensive way in me, and lead me in the way everlasting" (Ps. 139:23-24).

I'm a perfectionist, want everything done well *yester-*

day. Magazines don't arrive in the mail, and I fire off a complaint. I call on subcontractors, demand to know why I can see a carpet's seam, complain that a valance board ripples away from the wall.

I try to remember, "I'm a Christian; I must turn the other cheek. Smile." Instead, I let folks know, "I want it done right!"

"So, I was some snappish," I admit. "But at least I got results." A couple of years ago, however, I outdid myself and was called up short.

"You blew it!" a colleague wrote. "Several of us have been trying to witness to those people, but now . . ."

I'd written ugly words on paper, made the Lord look bad.

I fired off a letter of apology and discovered furious words are impossible to retract.

Today I can't say I've altogether changed. I'm still dealing with perfectionism and a short fuse. I still think everything should be done yesterday. But when I'm tempted to wage war, I make myself recall: I became a stumbling block for people who needed the Lord.

Today I don't make a phone call or write a letter of complaint without reminding myself, "Pray first; 'see if there be any wicked way in me . . . set a watch . . . before my mouth'" (Pss. 139:24; 141:3, both KJV).

And because God is faithful, He does.

Movers and Shakers—or Lost?

"Don't envy the wicked. Don't covet his riches. For the evil man has no future; his light will be snuffed out" (Prov. 24:19-20, TLB).

Their faces had graced television screens on nearly every continent. And I, being flesh and blood, had occasionally wrestled with covetousness. How lucky they all were to be famous and rich, to have the world at their feet —or so I thought until the Saturday afternoon I spotted what the world referred to as "movers and shakers" in a local restaurant—and realized those who had my envy needed my sympathy instead.

A television czar and a bevy of movie stars appropriated a corner table, guarded and behind dark glasses that must have made the radiant afternoon seem the middle of the night. Like tumbling dominoes, diners turned, whispered, and gawked.

They're goldfish! I thought, shaking my head as I recalled an ugly headline on a scandal sheet at a supermarket checkout stand. I wondered how I, a person who likes her space and privacy, might respond to craning, bobbing necks. "How dreary to be somebody!" They couldn't cough, sneeze, transgress without stargazers harassing them. Would these celebrities, for the rest of their lives, be subjected to public ridicule? If I were in their shoes, weren't there things in my life I wouldn't want publicly shared?

Yes, on occasion, I'd entertained a desire to become famous for my work. So had Christian artist friends of mine. But did we really want to be stared at, scrutinized? And those jet-setters visiting our town. Slick magazines had *published* their sins and, at the same time, revered them as gods and goddesses. There'd also been detailed reports in so-called legitimate newspapers and magazines that these stars were ill-behaved, sin-loving snobs. In fact, hadn't I read they were atheists? If those reports were true, what then? Could exquisite trappings and unlimited cash buy them even one minute in one of the mansions the Lord's preparing for His own?

I glanced at the full-length furs on *their* backs as they

moved from restaurant to limousine. And, suddenly, *I* felt undeservedly rich.

When Is the Best Time to Pray for Our Children?

Lisa was late. I knew it the minute I stepped into the dimly lit entryway and peered into the office where the clock counted the minutes on the blue plaid wall. Because she'd worked at a local shop even before graduating from high school, I knew exactly how long it took her to travel, when she began work, and when the mall closed. I knew, too, how often I'd read lately of purse-snatching, robberies, and a rape. I knew my daughter, a pretty college junior, walked some distance to her car and possessed not one ounce of fear.

"Honey, please, couldn't you just have someone walk with you?" I'd asked. "Caution," I'd called it, not fear. "Won't you see if one of the other girls would like to car-pool?" I'd also mentioned the fact that our old car wasn't exactly in its prime anymore. I worried about her driving the dark roads home.

"Mom," she'd smile, "where's that faith you keep telling me about? Don't you suppose God just might keep an eye on me?"

She was right, of course. My head knew that. My heart knew it too. But the night the clock suggested Lisa had been detained, I panicked.

"Father," I wailed, "Lisa isn't home yet!"

His response was instant. It came in the form of a reminder. Not three Sundays earlier, our pastor had shared how we were to pray promises, not fears.

"Father," I began again. "You've always taken care of her. I thank You for that. Thank You, also, that even as I pray, You can place a hedge of protection around her, and I can believe she will be home safe and soon. Amen."

Five minutes passed. Then, 10. Now she was more than half an hour overdue. I glanced at the clock and asked Scotty if we might drive down the road a way and check.

Scotty just shook his head, as if to say, "When are you going to learn?" He was right. I'd driven down the road on other occasions, only to discover I'd worried for absolutely nothing.

I reminded myself of the words I'd just prayed. I tugged my robe around me, ran my fingers through my hair, repeated my praises for Lisa's safety, felt a tightness in my chest and throat, drank water—and heard our old hatchback round the corner and enter our drive.

Exclaiming to my spouse all the way down the hall, I bounded down the stairs two at a time and met Lisa at the garage door, my eyes wide, while hers suggested disappointment that I'd "done it again."

"Honey," I said, feeling disappointed in myself but needing to know. "You're a little bit late. Was there a problem or—"

"I know, Mom," Lisa said, slipping her arm around my shoulders like a coach about to tell his Little Leaguer why he missed the final pitch. "There was this accident."

What followed was a complete description of a car-truck collision that had taken place just two automobiles ahead of hers. At an intersection where the lighting is poor and stop signs are barely heeded, a truck had plowed into a vehicle. It had taken firefighters and ambulance personnel to pull the injured out. Traffic had backed up for blocks. It looked as if a number of people had been seriously hurt.

Together, we walked to the den where my husband read. Lisa retold the details of the accident. Scotty said he'd known she'd be home soon and gave me a look from beneath a furrowed brow. But, then, I suddenly realized something about the *timing* was off.

"Honey," I said, dropping to sit beside my husband in his chair. "When I prayed a hedge around Lisa . . . well, it was 10 minutes *past* the time she'd have been at that corner. The accident would already have taken place, so I guess my prayers *didn't* cover her . . . It doesn't make sense," I said.

"What makes you think so?"

"I looked at the clock."

"Which one? The one on your office wall?"

"Yes," I said, feeling more than a little confused.

"Well, Babe, didn't you know? You've got to buy a new one or set back the hands on that thing once in a while. It's off—10 minutes fast."

As I moved to my room to correct the mistake, I knew tonight's timing hadn't been off at all. Every detail—even my lesson about trust and placing our children in our Father's hands—had been according to God's schedule all along. That the clock I'd considered trustworthy had proved imperfect only emphasized what God tells us in His Word. Our times *are* in His hands. So, too, is the time allotted to our kids.

Jesus Prayed for Himself

"Glorify your Son, that your Son may glorify you" (John 17:1). Jesus prayed for himself but did so because God would be glorified and others would be drawn to Him as Jesus completed the work His Father had given Him to do.

Recently, I began to notice that when friends prayed, answers came. Or I'd see someone's need, I'd pray, and I'd see the other person blessed. So one morning in my journal I wrote, "But what about me? How long must *I* wait?"

How long had it been since I'd prayed in earnest for my needs *and* that the answers might glorify Him?

I picked up a devotional from my desk and read, "God desires that we expect our requests to be answered." But is it OK for us to pray for ourselves? our needs? our desires?

Yes, Jesus did.

Time of Crisis: Time for Change

They summoned my husband as he arrived for work; he'd been selected to serve on an international team. Would he consider going to the Middle East? leave his family behind?

I called my prayer chain. We also prayed at home. Though newspapers were reporting terrorism, hijackings, and deaths, Scotty wasn't afraid. It wouldn't be his first assignment in an unfamiliar, unpredictable place. There'd been other teams, other countries halfway around the world. When he'd accepted former assignments, I'd worried and he'd been fine. Except for what, in retrospect, seemed minor problems, we'd both managed. God had covered all things well.

The following morning we decided: Scotty would take the assignment and would leave in a matter of weeks. I admit I did give in to a few tears, but God would take care of us, wouldn't He? And the loneliness? It wouldn't get to me this time. This time I wasn't prepared, however, for the next telephone call.

Our daughter, a junior in college, had been dealing with homesickness almost from the first day of her freshman year. There'd been telephone talks and lots of tears, but she'd determined to stay on the West Coast while my husband's work had situated us back east. Not one week after our decision regarding Scotty's going overseas, our daughter was calling again. "Mom," she cried, "I don't know what's happening. I feel like I'm freaking out."

She wasn't going to classes, couldn't go to work, had no interest in eating, didn't know what she wanted to do with her life. In five days, my husband and I were scheduled for an anniversary flight to Yugoslavia. But within the hour, Scotty had ironed my clothes, I'd packed, and just before midnight, I headed for Seattle, my daughter, and all that would have to be shipped home.

We withdrew Lisa from school, moved her from her living quarters, hauled 13 boxes to UPS, caught another red-eye special, and headed home to pack or to change our minds about our anniversary getaway.

Once home, it seemed God had covered even this dilemma. Lisa's friend, Debbie, had decided she wanted to sit out a semester too. She'd house-sit and talk with Lisa. Neither of the girls felt it would be a problem. In fact, they were looking forward to the time alone. So, Scotty and I flew out as scheduled, thinking all was well. By the time we arrived home, however, Lisa seemed even more confused. And so was I. I'd come home ill and went in for tests; the doctor promised medication would make me well within the week, but I couldn't seem to snap back. I'd worn out.

"Honey," I suggested, giving my daughter a hug, "how about you relaxing—and I will too. We'll talk anytime you want and for all of the time you want. You can see your friends, go to school here where we are, or quit. We'll re-do your room or help you find an apartment of your own. It'll all work out." My hopeful outlook lasted until about noon—when my husband called.

"Babe, I think you'd better sit down," he said. "I have something to tell you that you aren't going to like very much."

I wasn't liking much of anything I'd heard recently.

"We just got a call from national headquarters," he said. "They're closing our offices . . . for good."

For weeks we'd heard rumors, but none of us had really believed anyone could do anything so unthinking and unfair. But the rumor had become fact. My husband would be losing his job. Would positions open up somewhere else? It was something they couldn't yet say for sure.

The news seemed more than Lisa could bear. She'd come home to regroup and to rest in a place where she felt secure. Now we were either pulling up roots again—or joining the unemployed. This wasn't what she'd expected. She cried. I cried too.

That evening Scotty tried to reassure us. I tried to reassure him too. Lisa tried to make quick decisions about jobs, getting out on her own, buying a car, going to school at night. But the harder we tried, the worse we all felt. Tempers flared, tears flowed. Even the cat stayed out of our way. Lisa said she never should have come home! I exclaimed that I'd never have roots! And Scotty suggested we all settle down and pray. So, we did. In fact, as the days wore on, we prayed often. And we praised, even when words barely came. We made plans for "in case," argued with our circumstances and, sometimes, one another. But we also began noticing change: we were actually beginning to rest and to accept. Although there were still occasional outbursts, Lisa was becoming strong—so strong that one evening she said she had something she needed to say.

"I always felt guilty for going away to school and leaving you, Mom." She said she'd been torn between the East and the West, longed for independence, but had great difficulty seeing what required studies had to do with future and career. Now, however, since we'd been tossed into deep waters, she'd decided to swim. She realized, though we would always be Mom and Dad and wherever we were would be home, she was ready to sprout wings of her own.

Lisa's reflections and decision opened the door to Scotty's and my sharing some feelings of our own.

First, without saying the words, I'd led Lisa to believe I couldn't stand to see her go, and I was sorry for that. Actually, I'd come to like midlife, looked forward to this season with my spouse, wanted to try some new things, even experienced relief that Scotty and I could be a couple again.

Next, my husband shared that he, too, was glad to be moving on, that he might even enjoy trying his hand at other work. If his employer provided another slot, he would stay on. But, if the door closed completely, he would look to the Lord and do something else. Employed or no, all three under the same roof or apart, we knew God was not only in control but loving us. We were family—uprooted, relocated, rearranged.

I never imagined it could be so until it happened to us, but crisis had birthed not only change but also peace.

Lisa returned to school in the spring. She felt she knew what she wanted, where she was headed. She no longer felt guilty. Her trust in God had deepened. She knew, now, *we* were not her roots.

My husband did go to the Middle East, and I was left behind. But because of what we'd talked through, I was no longer apprehensive—not about the possibility of unemployment, nor about my daughter's living so far away. Though the times had been difficult, they had also been good. We'd become ready for whatever—miles apart, tightly knit.

The Trust

While working in a junior high a number of years ago, I was chosen to become the pilot teacher for a drug education program. As a result, I'd been sent to California for a two-week course where much of our training focused on a central theme: getting into the young addict's skin in order to better understand his makeup. We were told addicts trusted no one. In fact, we learned that most, long before they become addicted, have given up completely on trust.

"They no longer look for someone they can believe in," the director explained. "They don't even believe in themselves." Then he added, "We're going to involve you in an activity that should reveal just how much trust *you* have—*if* you will relinquish your control and allow us to teach you."

In the next hour, I would not only learn much about the addict but discover something about myself as well.

Once the introductory instructions were given, we were taken outside, lined up, and paired off. One partner was given a blindfold, the other was given the trust. The blindfolded partner was expected to take the arm of the near stranger, wander in and out of buildings, and then board a teetering, dilapidated bus for a ride around dark and unfamiliar grounds.

At first, I thought the adventure sounded like great fun. I wouldn't mind leading someone around. But then they fitted *me* with the blindfold—and instantly, I knew I wasn't going to like this. I doubted the partner they'd given me was going to watch out for a total stranger, and I knew he probably was going to let me break my neck! No longer was he a fellow teacher, someone I could respect. Suddenly, his intentions were suspect, and I refused to believe he would lead me through or around whatever dangerous obstacles were "out there." Only after many false starts and arguments did we manage to move forward and complete the project.

Back inside my room I couldn't sleep. I tossed, walked from window to washbasin, and considered the evening's experience. More than a dozen times I'd quizzed my guide, questioned his integrity, refused to take one more step, threatened to remove my blindfold. Now, as I sat alone in my room and enjoyed the warmth and security, I thought, "Father, I've been like that with You, too . . . always preferring to walk by sight, not faith." On numerous occasions God's "still small voice" had cautioned, but I hadn't listened—so certain was I that I could find the better way on my own.

Years later, I wonder if I've progressed much. I know I'm to trust Him for what I cannot see. When our daughter was away at school, there was the worry about money for tuition and airline tickets. More than once there'd been talk about eliminating the agency that employs my spouse. I get excited about new adventures, then lose heart, fear failure, and shut down. But, then I remember the blindfold and the training. I remember that what man can do for me, God can do even better.

I may *feel* as if I'm in the dark, but my God is not. I may *feel* as if I'm lost, but God knows exactly where I'm going and why. And, though my path *feels* rocky, He won't let me stumble or fall.

A safe journey is assured—so long as we allow Him to direct each of our steps. It's simply a matter of giving Him the trust.

His Word Have I Hidden in My Heart

I first memorized Scripture as a child. Back then it seemed one of those assignments teachers think up just to keep kids occupied. Today I'm adamant about recording Scripture verses on 3" x 5" cards. The cards can go with me anywhere, can be read and reread. Today I declare, "It is written," with confidence because I know what God's Word says *and* does.

I was doing the teaching when the Lord began to say something about ministering to women. I seldom join women's groups: How would I minister? I prayed, friends prayed. Before long, I understood I would write. Wonderful! I'd hide out at home with pot roasts simmering and windows opened to spring. "Yes!" I said, as I resigned my position and began. But nothing I wrote sold.

Then one Sunday our pastor said, "Scripture memorization isn't optional." It seemed as if God was doing the speaking and that the speech had something to do with me. I recalled Hab. 2:2-3. I was to stand on His promises until I saw my work in print. One year later two articles sold. Then, nothing—though I studied, attended workshops, and wrote every day.

"How long?" I cried—and discovered, "But as for you, be strong and do not give up, for your work will be rewarded" (2 Chron. 15:7). Today I look at my files and see nearly 700 articles placed along with two books. More "reward" than I'd been able to imagine when I first began.

Recently, my husband announced we might be moving again. We've been "moving again" for 17 years. For 7 years, I'd prayed to return to *this* place where we'd met and married. I'd stood on, "Go home to thy friends, and tell them how great things the Lord hath done for thee, and hath had compassion on thee" (Mark 5:19, KJV). Now my husband was thinking about moving us—*again?*

"No!" I wailed—until a friend called.

"You OK?" she asked.

"I am not!" During our last relocation, depression had all but consumed me. Now, before I'd half settled in, we might be packing up? I was certain I'd never again experience another creative moment, never see another Western mountain, never know the joy of life in a country town—until I recalled, "O Lord, I am oppressed; undertake for me" (Isa. 38:14, KJV); and "You will be like a well-watered garden, like a spring whose waters never fail" (58:11). No matter what the circumstances *seemed* to indicate, God was with me.

The next day, the promise I'd read was confirmed in the mouth of another. And I began to believe, "For the Lord your God is bringing you into a good land—a land with streams and pools of water, with springs flowing in the valleys and hills" (Deut. 8:7).

Did we move? We did. But long before the vans arrived, I had discovered, "'Leave your country and your people,' God said, 'and go to the land I will show you'" (Acts 7:3).

Scripture memorization has helped me in other areas of my life as well.

I grew up believing I never should have been born—until I discovered, "For I am fearfully and wonderfully made: marvellous are thy works; and that my soul knoweth right well" (Ps. 139:14, KJV). I'm one of God's works, am I not? So now, when the thought comes that I'm useless and will amount to no good, I shout, "For I am fearfully and wonderfully made!"

My husband was in the Middle East when the United States bombed Libya. Fear sickened me as I tried, for most of one night, to place a transatlantic call—wondering all the while if Scotty was safe. That terrifying night, the Lord quickened the verse, "With long life will I satisfy him" (Ps. 91:16).

Last week a friend called. Her son's leaving his wife and baby.

"I don't know what to do," she cried.

"Memorize Scripture," I said. "Find the promises for your kids—and for you."

We thanked God for His Word; and today at her desk or driving to work, facing problems beyond her own coping ability, my friend not only cries to the Lord but also recalls His words—words that have become wisdom, energy, and strength.

Does God's Word see us through just the big events in our lives? No! This morning, my husband and I "got up on the wrong side of bed." We don't know why. His speech had an edge to it; I snapped back. He asked, "What's the matter with you?" I said, "Nothing!" and whipped into the kitchen, jaws locked. Scotty backed the car out without "Love you." I wheeled into the house and slammed the door. Thirty minutes later, however, the Lord brought to mind, "Stop being . . . angry" (Eph. 4:31, TLB). And I turned to prayer.

God tells us if we'll confess our sins, He'll forgive and cleanse *and* enter into our predicament. I'd no sooner begun to pray and confess God's Word when Scotty called. He was sorry. I was sorry too. All is now well—because God's Word works!

This afternoon I opened my mailbox, expecting letters from friends, a check, or editors' acceptances. I found, instead, 33 rejected manuscripts, some held for five years. An editor had changed his mind. And the enemy began to hiss, "You're wasting your time; why don't you give up?" But I recalled, "'For I know the plans I have for you,' declares the Lord, 'plans to prosper you . . . to give you hope and a future'" (Jer. 29:11). With my 3" x 5" cards in my hand I shouted thoughts from the Scriptures: "You will be like a well-watered garden! Slowly, surely it shall all come to pass! God's Word *never* returns to Him void! His Word have I hidden in my heart!"

And you know what? His Word was given for every one of us—for you, for me, for all. "For God so loved the *world*" (John 3:16, emphasis added).

So, it's looking like a bad day? Look up, hide His Word in your heart. It never returns to Him void.

The Sunset

Standing on tiptoe, the muscles taut in the backs of my legs, I peered out through my kitchen window, trying to catch more than a thin glimpse of the pink and plum sky. But the six-foot fence and concrete block wall surrounding our backyard interfered. No matter how I strained, I could see only a small, radiant patch of color.

Looking up, I caught sight once more of the grand homes on the mountainside above our very ordinary neighborhood. Built with massive expanses of glass, sprawling patios, and immense balconies wrapped around the fronts and sides of those high-priced homes, the owners could take in the entire panorama any and every evening—no obstacles, no restrictions, none.

Envious, frustrated, grumbling under my breath, I turned from the window—and remembered the woman.

I hadn't seen her in our church before—not until the previous Sunday. We'd just entered the sanctuary and slipped into our seats when I caught sight of her wending her way down the crowded aisle. She was a tall, handsome woman with flaming auburn hair and a face as aglow as the New Mexico morning. Her pretty teenager had walked beside her. So, too, had her Seeing Eye dog.

The recollection struck me like a physical blow. I could feel my face flushing the crimson of the sunset. What wouldn't that woman give to see as I could, however restricted the view?

"Lord," I petitioned, kneeling right there by my sink, "forgive me for being so quick to complain and so slow to acknowledge the gifts and blessings with which You have filled my life. Thank You, Father, for the miracle of sight, so undeserved and too often taken for granted. Thank You for the love of beauty You've instilled in me, for the awe and joy I feel when confronted with the magnificence of what You've created for us."

Standing, I surveyed our very ordinary house in our very ordinary neighborhood, and added a prayer of thanks for a glimpse of a miraculous, setting sun and for a much-needed look at myself.

The Older I Get . . .

"A man's wisdom gives him patience; it is to his glory to overlook an offense" (Prov. 19:11).

My husband and I had no sooner seated ourselves in our Sunday School class than our teacher said, "The older we get, the more trouble we have with envy, I think." He wasn't telling me anything I didn't already know! I'd been dealing with envy and indignation for weeks! First, a writer *half* my age had been featured in our local paper. Why? Because not only did he support himself with his work, but his books had been acclaimed by the toughest critics in the publishing world. Then, I'd no sooner decided not to envy the young novelist than the biggest bookstore in our small town ran a full-page ad: All local authors would be in the store on a Saturday to autograph their books.

"Why isn't your name here?" my sister asked.

Though both of my books were currently selling, I hadn't been invited. You can call it imagination, but I suspected I hadn't been included because my books were Christian, not secular.

To add to my frustration, my spouse is a fly fisherman, and his favorite expert would be signing books in that store! An autographed copy of the author's prized work would make Scotty's year! "But I can't go into that place . . . I'm mad, mad, mad!"

"You should go," my sister said. "How many opportunities are you going to have to get this man's signature?"

"Oh, great. You always were the manipulator in the family," I said, knowing it wasn't true, but frustrated and wanting to vent anger at someone, and knowing I'd best not enter the bookstore and tell the manager a thing or two. So I attended the party, got the signature, watched the store's owner wrap my gift, and, silently vowing I would not address the affront, returned to my parked car, where I slammed the door so hard my ears popped.

"Lord, if You think I need a lesson in humility—"

"Yes, as a matter of fact—"

"I don't! I'm humble. I'm a Christian. My writing is good." The day would come when this woman would groan, "To think I had a chance to introduce her in my store . . ."

It took more than a year before I could admit what I'd heard in my spirit was the truth: I had needed the lesson—and the others that followed. Pride does not please our Father; humility is His plan.

Whether we're writing, minding children, or managing the store, our entire social system seems bent on pitting us one against the other. Bent, also, on seeing to it we Christians feel we're second-rate. But that Saturday afternoon I made myself a promise: Though the older I get the more difficult it seems, I will run my race with patience, overlook offenses, and remember humility comes before honor.

Are You a Success? Am I?

The older I get, the more I wrestle with the word *success*. Joseph, whose story is told in Genesis, was certainly recognized as a success *after* Pharaoh appointed him second only to himself. But wasn't Joseph also successful in the pit? in the dungeon? because he continued to trust God in what must have seemed unsuccessful surroundings and circumstances? Scripture tells us, "The Lord was with Joseph and gave him success in whatever he did" (Gen. 39:23). Sounds to me as if that meant *while* he was in prison too.

In 2 Pet. 1:5-8 (TLB), the writer says if we'll work hard to be good, learn to know God better, discover what He wants us to do, put aside our own desires, become patient and godly, and gladly let God have His way, we will grow spiritually. But it also says we'll "become fruitful." Can we separate the two?

A number of years ago, my husband and I joined a church where we were taught to plant seeds and reap harvests—that abundance, pleasure without pain, and even luxury could be ours if we were truly walking in, standing on, and believing God's Word.

Yahoo! After years of plodding, we would be reveling in wealth once we got the principles down!

I began to push in my work. On my office wall, I tacked pictures of homes surrounded by acres of land. I dreamed of writing blockbuster novels, of building a lodge-like home on the water where my children and grandchildren would congregate. I would travel and gift my husband with a horse, a llama, a workshop of his own. Scotty, though more reserved than I, began also to persevere in overtime, plant seed, and believe. And, together, we waited and wondered why *our* ship hadn't come in, while other church members were building larger storehouses, rejoicing in their wealth.

"Claim more, claim louder. Believe more, believe and shout!" we were told. One friend advised us to add action to our words. She'd been trying on mink coats, Cadillacs, and a Mercedes-Benz. Both her church and the business in which she'd invested advocated such rehearsals for success. "Say what you desire to see actualized in your life, and what you say you'll have!" my friend declared.

Scripture does, in a way, seem to support such beliefs—scriptures such as "Ye have not, because ye ask not" (James 4:2, KJV); and "All these things shall be added unto you" (Matt. 6:33, KJV); and "Whatsoever ye shall ask in my name . . ." (John 14:13, KJV).

So why weren't *we* moving forward? Why weren't *we* amassing fortunes, collecting automobiles, designer fashions, and pleasure boats?

On the heels of my wondering and doubts, I read a Chuck Colson interview. In it, he shared his transformation and his turning to Christ after his involvement with Watergate and his imprisonment. "Events in Colson's life," Tim Martindale wrote, "have served only to reinforce the message that life and success are fragile things that must be used and appreciated with great care and gratitude." And I asked myself, had my husband and I realized the sort of success *we'd* been seeking, would *we* have given it great care? shown proper gratitude? Or was there yet much maturing of the soul to be accomplished in us? And what about our goal setting? Hadn't we set goals based on envy, jealousy, desires to have what belonged to someone else?

Henry David Thoreau wrote, "Why should we be in such desperate haste to succeed? . . . If a man does not keep pace with his companions, perhaps it is because he hears a different drummer."

That was it! We weren't falling behind. It was just that we were marching to a different drummer. Still, if we didn't pursue and strive and attain, what then would the Christians in our "successful" church think of us? That we lacked initiative or sufficient faith? Again, I found my answers in God's Word, in the reflections of wise men—and in the lives of several special friends.

Two Scripture passages became immediately important to me. First, "Hezekiah trusted in the Lord . . . held fast to the Lord . . . did not cease to follow him . . . kept the commands . . . and . . . was successful in whatever he undertook" (2 Kings 18:5-7); and second, "Have faith in the Lord your God and you will be upheld; have faith in his prophets and you will be successful" (2 Chron. 20:20). Hezekiah's mark of success? He'd trusted in and held fast to the Lord and kept His commands.

Aleksandr Solzhenitsyn wrote, "I came to realize that the object of life was not prosperity, as we are made to believe, but the maturing of the soul." Benjamin Disraeli said, "The secret of success is constancy to purpose." Reading these words, I thought about three of my friends.

Because illnesses and surgeries had begun to produce bills her husband couldn't handle by himself, one friend was asked by her husband if she would consider going to work. Today, she's proudly cleaning houses because she's purposed to help her mate shoulder the financial burden in their home. According to Jer. 4:1-2 (TLB), a good testimony equals success. So can my housecleaning friend be considered successful? Jeremiah seems to say so.

A second friend's adult daughter burned out. This friend, though she was loving her empty nest and time with her husband alone, prepared a room, rearranged her work schedule, and made herself available for those times when her daughter would need to talk. Isn't this mother's testimony equal to success?

And what about my friend who supported her husband's dream even when it meant no roots for years? Now that her husband's a millionaire, is he the success? Or could success be attributed to the wife who stood by her husband when there were only sleeping pallets on rented floors?

I dream of writing best-sellers. I desire success. If I come to the end of my life and have not realized my dream, will I have fallen short? Isn't success listening for God's voice, seeking and making every effort to do His will? Isn't success advancing confidently along the path He's set for me, for you? Isn't it praising Him, expressing our gratitude for who He is and for what He's done in our lives? reaching out to others? walking in the direction of our dreams, yes, but giving our wills in exchange for His—even if we fail?

I don't judge fellow Christians who believe for mink and who wear it in their Cadillacs. But, I've had to face myself and ask some hard questions, have been forced to admit I was seeking self-indulgence—not what might be God's idea of success. Oh, I believe it is His will that I press on and believe for what He's planned for me. But, I also believe today it may not be His plan that I drive a

Mercedes-Benz (though I surely would like to), that I amass material goods or garner applause. These things may be added unto me. But I am to purpose to seek His face, His will for my life, to run the race where and how He says, "Run!"

I'm not putting down the kind of success that's synonymous with financial prosperity. I'm flesh and blood, so some days I long for that too. But if, one day, our dreams—yours and mine—do come true, I believe we will have actually become successful the hour we decided to trust, obey, and draw close to God.

The Act of Quietly Waiting

My seventh graders had experienced great difficulty comprehending certain parts of speech, especially the verb.

"A verb is an action word," I explained. However, when I suggested "believe" and "wait" were also action words—just like "jump," "scurry," and "wrestle"—my students announced they didn't understand.

"But it's so simple!" I exclaimed. "You don't have to *see* the activity for there to *be* activity."

Then one morning I became the student and realized I was just as confused, in some respects, as the kids in my class.

On Saturday mornings, my husband and I enjoyed doughnuts and coffee out. Normally, it was a time for each of us to share our past week's happenings—though occasionally we weren't quite awake enough to talk. This particular morning we weren't quite awake. In addition, I was unsettled about matters I'd taken to the Lord. Unsettled because I'd decided He hadn't listened to any one of my appeals.

Silent, I began watching a boy in his late teens who was waiting for a bus. He waited, however, by walking from the corner, back to the doughnut shop, over to the opposite corner, into a service station, back to the cross-walk, and, at one point, into and through the intersection. By the time his bus arrived on schedule, the boy was obviously worked up, exhausted, annoyed.

"That's pathetic!" I exclaimed to my husband. "I don't believe what I just watched. That boy had a schedule in his hand, his bus wasn't one bit late, and he hadn't hurried it by pacing from pillar to post." I shook my head, frowning. "What a ridiculous way to wait."

"Oh?" Scotty grinned. "Really?"

What did he mean, "Really"? Why the silly grin on his face? "Yes, *really*," I said.

"But isn't that exactly what *you* do . . . even when it's God *himself* who's saying, 'Wait'?" He shook his head, grin still in place.

"No way," I said, trying not to laugh. But even as I protested, I knew he was right. How often had I decided my having to wait could only mean God was doing nothing? How many times had I decided—because I saw nothing happening in the physical realm—nothing was happening, period?

As I sipped hot coffee, I had to admit I could remember several instances when it became obvious God was *trying* to teach me how to wait. Frantically, I'd petitioned Him for a promotion and a transfer for my husband, but I hadn't hurried it up by one single day. The promotion and move had arrived in His own time.

On our house-hunting trip, I'd paced a path in the motel carpet because houses were either priced beyond our means or falling apart. But we'd found just the home for us, hadn't we—in God's time?

I'd been ill for years, but as God had promised, I'd been healed completely—and at the perfect time and place.

Seldom, looking back, could I say I'd waited calmly. More often than not, I'd waited like the boy at the bus stop. And just as he hadn't rushed the driver, neither had I hurried God.

As we walked toward our car, I said, "You know, Honey, you're right. It's no wonder I haven't been able to get 'waiting' across to my students. I'm still learning to understand the meaning of the word myself." I laughed. "But Monday I'm going to give it another try."

Scotty opened my door, and I slipped into the passenger's seat. "Waiting is a verb," I said, "and a verb is an action word. But Scripture says, 'It is good both to hope and wait quietly for the salvation of the Lord'" (Lam. 3:26, TLB).

Scotty backed from our parking space. I touched his arm. "And you just wait and see," I said. "I'll not only teach those kids about waiting, but we're going to start learning about adverbs too—we're going to begin with 'quietly.'"

This Is the Day!

We'd been planning this day for a year—ever since we'd returned from the last farm show where a Guernsey had delivered her calf and, two stalls over, a spindly colt mesmerized a speechless crowd.

"Can't wait!" I whooped, bounding from our bed. Today was going to be special! One to share in future epistles to family and friends.

Within minutes (miraculously) I'd showered, dressed, and perfumed. Scotty poured steaming coffee into travel mugs. And we pulled out, celebrating a blueing Pennsylvania sky.

"Won't make it to Montana today," I laughed, "but at least we're headed west."

"Yup."

"I like you," I said. "You don't mince words."

In the middle of our township, I discovered my hair wasn't yet dry. I hung my head upside down to where hi-lo heat finished what I hadn't taken time for at home. I hadn't taken time, because we'd stayed up too late. But who could resist an evening with South Dakota friends, roast beef, and a table game?

On the turnpike, Scotty slipped Patsy Cline into the tape deck. I hoped he'd soon tire of her; then I'd select something piano with the sound of rain and flute—something to transport me to the city where sloops skim Puget Sound—where whitecaps and gulls escort ferries to islands, gourmet ice cream, and extravagant views of Mount Rainier. I admitted something good *could* be said about horse country. "It's stable," I said, enjoying my pun— while my spouse pretended not to hear a word I'd said.

Alongside the highway, cows ambled from one cluster of trees to the next. "The pace is sweet out here," I said, slipping my hand through Scotty's plaid-shirted arm.

"Yup."

You may not be wordy, I thought, glancing at my cowboy who seemed to fill the car, but I always know where you stand.

On either side of the turnpike, it was deciduous. In a clearing, there were white farms, blue silos, Amish children at play. The grass wasn't yet green, but rooftops were.

There was wash on the lines: blue, maroon, the color of coal.

Church spires graced the horizon. Then, suddenly, a tract of faddish homes assaulted the terrain. Where pastures once pleased the eye, road signs advertised manufacturer's outlets, beer gardens, and farm machinery.

Raised in the city, I thought, but I'm tempted to mount a protest about the so-called progress they're making out here. Where will farms and farmers go when we've plastered the land with prefab condominiums? Will anyone visit a neighbor for checkers and apple pie? When we've planted chemical companies in cornfields, who will remember what security was? Where once there were stands of trees, earthmovers had driven the deer and ruffed grouse out. Where will we take our families for Sunday drives? Where would skiffs of snow and squirrels and the red fox go?

"I'll be glad when we get there," I said, pressing close to my spouse. "I can't wait to see the rabbits and goats."

I relaxed against the seat's back, and Scotty pointed to a farm with a stone house and a clump of pink pigs. "They're actually clean animals, given a chance to be so," he said.

I wondered if people were like that too. Did anyone really want to wallow in litter and fear of the strangers next door?

Crows began to glean a field, while a German shepherd contemplated running them off. A barn the color of ripe corn materialized; a burro dined on a nibble of hay.

"Never saw such wonderful things in the city," I said.

As we passed the exit marked "Mount Hope," I remembered potato doughnuts. The year before, we'd discovered church members cooking and waiting in hungry lines. This year, we'd made a pact: no "Geedunks." This year, we'd head straight for the booths where everything would be home style and incredible!

"Full speed ahead!" I cheered.

On the south side of the road, where trees topped low slopes, there were stretches of shadows and snow. To the north, spring! In the distance, a snaky wire fence framed a field.

"We must be getting close to the city, though," I said, glowering at billboard ads for cheap motels and fast foods. "I'm acquiring a horse-and-buggy mentality," I said.

Within minutes, we were surrounded by road equipment, lumberyards, new cars, and cars that had become debris.

Earth had been pilfered from a slope where birch once reflected sunlight and dressed up what was now grotesque. Motorists sounded horns like barking dogs. Rusted machinery and a tower of tires welcomed visitors to the state's capital.

"Progress Avenue," I read aloud. "Sure," I murmured, pondering the blight.

"Well, Babe, we're almost there," Scotty said.

"Thank goodness," I whispered, adding a prayer of relief that we'd soon delight in a more fit habitat.

Rounding a bend, Scotty signaled for a left. "One good thing about our getting a late start," he said, "most folks will have gone home."

"Most folks?" I shrieked—and Scotty braked. But for one lone pickup and an Airstream, we were looking at an empty parking lot and a bulletin tied to a post. The farm show had closed—yesterday.

"Babe . . ." Scotty squeezed my hand. "You had your heart set on something special."

"It has been special," I said, giving him a hug. "I had a chance to do some thinking. You know how I sometimes grumble about all the 'urban' things I miss?"

Scotty nodded.

"Well, this morning I'm thinking maybe 'country's' beginning to grow on me."

Scotty smiled. "Then, how about I show you some more of it?" He turned the truck around. "We'll search out some unpaved roads," he said. And, we did. Off the main highway, we discovered barns with church windows, a family's graveyard, and a hand-hewn sign in a farmer's yard: "This is the day which the Lord hath made; we will rejoice and be glad in it" (Ps. 118:24, KJV).

"Yes. We will," we avowed.

Up ahead, a buggy with its trotter at the helm headed for home. Alongside the road, we spotted shocks of corn stacked to dry, a sign for bread, and brown eggs.

It hadn't been the day we'd planned, but it had been good, all the same. And, over shoofly pie in a country diner, we rejoiced.

Winter Wheat

In Montana, in November, very few are "thinking snow" because the snow has *already* arrived, and many are *already* grumbling and hiding out in the house. When we lived in Montana, come November 1 was *already* wondering, What about spring? I'd head for the mailbox, unable to see the road. Snow would drift down inside my collar, up under my glasses, and into my shoes. "Will summer come?" I'd grumble. "Will I ever be warm again?" I'd decide the weather was responsible for everything wrong in my life. "I doubt anything I'm hoping for will ever come to pass," I'd say. But, then, I'd remember the farmer down the road.

Only weeks earlier, our neighbor had stood waist-high in tall and nodding grain, his straw hat tipped back as he studied a field west of his barns. He'd cut the eastern field, but it was obvious—as he walked slow, all the while stroking his chin—he was trying to decide: "This one? ready for harvest or no?"

I remember thinking how like that field I felt. A friend—one who only months before had asked how to head a manuscript, which computer to buy, what professional magazines to read—had called to announce she'd sold her first book, received an advance greater than all my pay for the entire year! Furthermore, she'd mentioned the several books in her closet, and the editor had said, "Send them all!"

"Give me a break!" I whooped. What about me? I thought. Had God forgotten I'd studied, prayed, worked hard for eight years?

Driving into town, I remembered the farmer could look at one field and know it was ready—look at another and know it had growing to do. It was harvesttime for my friend, not me.

Several days later, I spotted another field—one planted to winter wheat. Scotty says the seedlings lie dormant under the snow. They're waiting to produce crops *next* year—after the earth has warmed, after the rain. And I wonder why we give in to impatience and comparisons. We see one blessed and another lifted up and we ask, "What about me?" We earn degrees, persevere in our work, and wonder why the boss hasn't noticed us. We become room mothers, Brownie leaders, directors of kids' choirs, and, for our troubles, see our own children walk away not only from us but from God. We drive meals on wheels, squeeze in time to work at perfecting our gifts, and we wait.

Today, with winds biting and summer on my mind and the New Year two calendar pages away, I know I'm to give thanks this season for the other writer's crop—to also give thanks for God's timing, for His knowing who is ready and who is not—and in my heart I celebrate for my friend. I resolve not to look back fretting. I resolve to thank Him even for failures because at least He's taught me to try.

Yes, in the midst of winter, it seems odd to be thinking summer sunshine, summer fields. But we must. I admit it isn't easy. Some days I think I've taken two steps forward and more than one step back. But even while I'm feeling left out, in the dark—about as happy as those seedlings must feel under two feet of snow—the choice is mine. I can wrestle and fret and complain—or I can rest.

Like many of you, I'm feeling like winter wheat. I'm waiting on the Husbandman, hoping I will yet see a fruitful harvest when it's time. I'm learning to walk through the wintry, stinging times, and I'm learning to trust while I wait.

HANG ON...

You came near when I called you,
and you said, "Do not fear."

LAM. 3:57

When Doors Begin to Close

Earlier this evening, before my husband left for another one of those meetings that turns his workday into 13 hours instead of 8, we talked. At our house, this "talking" frequently means I unload while Scotty tries to hear what I'm working through now.

It isn't easy for me to admit feeling depressed, disillusioned, in the dark about God—what He's up to and why—whether He's punishing, or if this is simply a test. I'm supposed to be "inspirational"—upbeat, happy, praising, overflowing with words of faith. But today I was down. Actually, I couldn't remember the last time I'd awakened chirping, ready not only to face the morning but to tackle it with gusto and joy.

For weeks (be honest—it's been months) I'd struggled with the "Whys." Why, though I'd spent hours and years working at my work, was I still coming up short? Scotty would retire in just seven years. Without my help, would we be able to build our dream home? return to the part of the world we loved? know that our needs would be met? I had expected my writing to become income by now, but that had not been the case.

"Everything I try seems to be failing. Even the doors once open to me are beginning to shut," I declared while Scotty ate leftovers (how long had it been since I'd really cooked?). "I don't understand," I moaned; "I don't."

"No?" My husband tucked my hands into his. "Well, tell me this, Babe: do you remember, in Pennsylvania, when the starling got in through the fireplace and you called the office because you didn't know what to do?"

Boy, did I! I'd panicked, thought the thing was going to die, wondered if I should run outside and wait for Scotty to come home or call 911!

"Do you also remember the only way to save it was to close every door and window in the house but one?"

Only one door open? Yes! That's what Scotty had suggested. So, I'd closed windows, pulled shades, and shut all doors but for a slider. Then I swung the fireplace glass wide (my eyes closed), and the crazed bird had flown out and into the center of the room, flapped its sooty wings all over my carpet and couch, and then, with a glad squawk, ascended toward the light and out into the summer sun. If I'd given him a choice of windows and doors, the bird might have become confused, beaten its wings against walls and ceiling, worn itself out, and died. But all but one route had been closed; there'd been only one clear way open to him. The best way, the way not only out of his dilemma but into a wide and beautiful soaring place.

"Could it be?" Scotty whispered, his eyes grinning and warm, "that's just exactly what God's doing? Shutting every door but the door, the plan He has for you? Because it's time for *you* to fly—free to write what you've been wanting to say for a long, long time—free to be what it is He has on His mind for you?"

It was true. There was a book within me that longed to be written—joys, disappointments, times the Lord had blessed me, days when I'd walked through darkness and discovered He was there. Yet so long as all sorts of passageways remained open, I'd allow myself to dabble—a little of this, a little of that. But one morning I'd shut up every avenue of escape but for one to a starling. Was it possible God was also closing every door but His to me? Was He saying, "Follow the light I've provided for you so that I can lead you to where you'll be able to try *your* wings?"

Tonight, with my husband away and the house quiet, I've renewed my vow to believe the seeming dead ends are for my own good—that if I'll simply trust and follow, I will one day know again the joy of flight.

Tonight I'm thinking how He wants, also, to open doors for you, though you, like me, may only see right now doors that are closing or have already closed. God says in His Word He has perfect plans for you and for me, plans for good and not for evil, plans to take each of us from the place where we are confused—that we might soar on the wings He has given us, that we might also know the joy of mounting up on wings as eagles in His will.

I don't love starlings. I never have. Actually, I think they're about the most obnoxious bird in the yard! But I cared when that bird became trapped in our fireplace. Just think how much more God cares about you.

He Kept in Touch

It had been nine agonizingly long weeks since Scotty's job had taken him to the back country in India where there were no phones and no mail deliveries. And though we'd agreed there was no point in trying to communicate, I desperately needed him now.

I recalled the morning he'd boarded the plane. "God *always* has His eye on us," he'd said when we'd prayed. "Trust Him. He'll keep us in touch."

For a while it seemed as if I'd make it through the lonely times. Now, however, it was the Fourth of July. Scotty was halfway around the world, my friends were vacationing with family, my daughter had plans with classmates, and I'd been left alone—but for Toby.

The first moment I saw him, I believed in love at first sight.

"Mom, he's only a cat!" my daughter laughingly scolded.

But mornings, Toby showered with me; days, he bossed the dog. I washed dishes; he swatted suds. While I ate breakfast, he begged for an egg of his own. Occasionally, he'd sneak to the neighbor's bird feeder; but when I pressed my nose against the window, he'd leap from his perch and, tail switching, strut across the lawn and through the back door as if to say, "Ho hum, I get so bored with those birds." Afternoons, he'd "help" me garden, sew, turn the pages of a book, and type. Nights, he'd purr us both to sleep.

When I'd feel lonely, Toby'd appear—fresh from some mischief, smiling—and I'd instantly feel *someone* cared.

One evening, however, when I returned from dinner out—alone—I discovered Toby limp behind the sofa. He couldn't strut or smile; he didn't even seem to know me.

I considered praying; but, recalling how often I'd begged the Lord for just one word from my husband, I clenched my jaws, cradled Toby, and raced to an emergency clinic across town. By the time I'd spent three hours (and $65.00 I couldn't afford), I knew: Toby was dying, and there was nothing going to change that.

"Feline leukemia," the veterinarian explained. "We can put him to sleep or give him steroids. Might last another couple of days if we do."

I forced composure. I had no intention of making a scene in the stranger-filled lobby. But my lips trembled as I choked out, "I just can't let you put him to sleep."

"Well, the steroid shots might—"

"No!" I erupted—surprising the attendant *and* myself. "Can't do that, either," I added, shaking my head.

Everyone fixed late-night stares on me.

"Besides, he's only a cat," I whispered into the peach

fur, shoving the door with my hip, laboring across the parking lot.

Hugging Toby as if I could keep him from dying by doing so, I nearly choked on asphalt fumes. "O God, You *say* You're always here, but . . ."

Though I was normally a rational thinker who knew it was the government who ordered husbands to places where they were out of touch, tonight I blamed God. I was also on the verge of condemning Scotty. His past encouragements seemed like Sunday School jargon, and his prayers seemed a poor substitute for his presence when I needed him so much.

"God," I wept, "it's been difficult enough without this. How could You allow . . . ?"

My body trembled violently. Aloud, I recalled weeks and weeks of extreme heat, depression, fear—and bills. Weeks of bearing one responsibility after another. I wondered if I'd ever stop crying.

"God! Where are You? It's been so long. I've had to make too many decisions alone. I need to talk things out!" Straining to focus on the rain-slick road, I gasped, "It isn't just Toby. This car's given me nothing but trouble, and there's a question about taxes. And You tell me—if You're my Provider—where am I supposed to come up with money enough for Lisa's dress?"

Broken—and with my kitten more still than I'd seen any living thing—I was empty. "Lord, I need Scotty," I wept, screaming through the mud-smeared windshield. "I *need* to talk to Scotty, and I need to talk to him *now!*" I repeated convulsively.

As I entered our dark house and settled Toby in a corner, I touched the top of his head and smoothed his fur. He didn't move, but I heard him sigh.

I slipped into my aged bathrobe, prepared myself a

cup of black coffee, and retreated into Scotty's overstuffed chair—just as the phone's shrill ring pierced the room.

As I raised the receiver to my ear, a faint, Oriental-sounding voice asked, "You will accept collect call from India?"

Would I? "Yes!" was all I could manage. I was too overcome to say more. My husband was on the line.

I cried. Scotty consoled. I sputtered. He understood. For 30 minutes, I shared everything, raised questions, openly spoke of my doubts. Scotty suggested answers and offered encouragement. With wisdom I knew was his gift from God, my husband relieved me of the pressures, the fears. He told me that in order to place this call, he'd made a reservation, hoping he'd actually pass through New Delhi at that time. Then he'd dealt with red tape, waited nearly three hours, stayed by the phone—and prayed.

"And prayed," I whispered, smiling. My husband had been right all along. God had accomplished "the impossible." He had kept us in touch.

Our God Is in Control

How difficult and confused our days seem to have become. War, rumors of war, famine, disease. And then, just about the time we're feeling we can put our fears behind us and hang on, the world shocks us with yet another slaughter, a hostage taken, a terrorist bomb.

On television and movie screens, in books and magazines, and even in our schools, we hear God mocked. It would appear the world is having its own way, that the Christ who hung on the Cross failed. Aligning ourselves with such a One often sets us up for ridicule. We're made to feel we're failures and that so long as we continue to worship Him, we'll continue to be considered odd, fall short. Even within the church community, some call out-and-out faith naive. But is any of this truly cause for alarm?

If we understand Revelation correctly and if we belong to Him, is there not cause for trust and joy? We read, "All nations will come and worship before you" (15:4). All. And where there is worship, will there not also be peace, an end to divisions and war?

God's Word says there's coming a day when He will take up the reins again and will rule. For that day, we must trust. When the promise in Revelation begins to sound improbable, then I must remind myself it's time to return to the prophets, to rediscover things and events promised years and years ago that have already come to pass. It is time to take a stand and to believe once again.

Today, I tune in a radio broadcast; tonight, I'll scan our local news. Cause for fear? No! God's Word is the last word. God's Word is the news I stand on. Only His ways are just and true. Only the King of the ages is holy. He alone will act righteously and bring the peace (Rev. 15:3-4).

For this good news—I can most definitely hang on.

The Harbinger

Scripture says, "Therefore judge nothing before the time, until the Lord come, who both will bring to light the hidden things of darkness, and will make manifest the counsels of the hearts: and then shall every man have praise of d" (1 Cor. 4:5, KJV). But not until our youngest began .aking plans to leave did I fully understand that promise.

Lisa had applied for and been accepted by six colleges and universities. She found the process both exciting and awesome; Scotty and I thought it was the pits! With each acceptance came an invitation to visit a campus. And, visit we did. To eastern Pennsylvania, then west, then north. But the more we gallivanted, the less Lisa seemed to understand about the need to make a final decision. She reveled in the "courting," while for our part, poring over loan applications and financial aid forms was beginning to drive us both nuts! Worse, we were beginning to wonder how in the world we were going to pay for the desire of our daughter's heart.

Several weeks into the adventure and in tears, I knelt before the Lord and told Him how our finances looked, what our needs were, and, to my surprise, that I didn't think I could stand it if my daughter traipsed all the way from Pennsylvania to Washington State. Not until I'd told Him how I felt did I actually realize how I felt—that Lisa's leaving was beginning to bother me more than our financial concerns.

"God," I cried, "what's happening to our family?"

"Don't you know I'm trying to bless you?" His thoughts within my own heart touched me as if He'd spoken out loud.

"Bless me?" I wailed, jumping to my feet and leaving my prayer closet more anxious than when I'd entered it. A blessing? My daughter 3,000 miles away from home?

Several days later, we decided to drive across the state to Pittsburgh. Lisa wanted to investigate just one more school.

Driving to the turnpike, we were surrounded by darkness except for the full moon that had begun to slip down behind the horizon ahead. There was no traffic and no sign of a light on either side of the road.

Silent, because Lisa slept, our previous night's conversation played itself out in my head. The discussion had centered on our daughter's apparent decision. Though I'd tried believing otherwise, it seemed certain she was going away. She would move to the other side of the country, leaving us behind. I couldn't understand it. So, again, I went to the Lord.

"Father," I whispered, "somehow I do sense You're trying to bless us, but I really don't understand how. I've tried to relax and trust You, tried to see it Your way, but I can't."

In the heart of me, I felt a sort of darkness—as dark as our surroundings until, with what was nearly a flash, our surroundings suddenly changed.

Without so much as a trickle of light to announce its rising, a radiant glow engulfed the valley beyond us and illumined the mountains we'd left behind. We were instantly warmed, and what had seemed a desolate land was, instead, an expanse of white farmhouses, red barns, cascading streams, Guernsey cows, and giant oaks.

At the sun's insistence, the darkness had disappeared. And in its place there was moving, growing, abounding life.

Craning my neck out the passenger window, I noted the moon still hovered, just as last evening's concern lingered with me; but in the new day's light, its power seemed much less ominous.

As the countryside warmed, the Lord began kindling my spirit, reigniting my faith. He would also shed light on my confusion, in due time. For now, He was encouraging me to rest and enjoy the dawn. No, I didn't yet understand, nor could I wholly accept that a Father who desired to bless me might take what I felt I could not give. But I did know His hand was over us all. Just as the new day's harbinger had displaced the darkness, there would come a day when His perfect timing would displace my despair.

This morning, as I sit in my study, I realize that new day has arrived. We lugged Christmas decorations to the attic yesterday. This morning, Lisa, now a sophomore in college, returned to Washington after what was a happy family break.

It's taken some time. Her leaving meant adjustment. But my daughter's becoming a woman. For Scotty and me, there's been change as well. We've grown personally, become a couple again, begun to examine and develop our gifts.

God, as He promised, has shed light on things once hidden in the dark. And it has been good.

Hearing Is Believing

"I tell you the truth . . . those who hear will live" (John 5:25).

She rests at my kitchen table, joy obvious in her comfortable laughter and in the way she relates the stories of her life—a husband who left her when she was 18, illness upon illness, comas, multiple surgeries, and now, the loss of her legs.

"Sometimes I ask myself," she says, "how it is I'm the only member of the family who's come to know the Lord."

My neighbor is one of more than a dozen children. All but my neighbor are involved in alcohol, battering, violence, and drugs. All but my neighbor are without hope.

"I've tried to tell them about Him," she adds. "But they just won't listen to a word I say."

It's plain to see—even as I help her to her new feet and we make our way to the door—my neighbor has both listened and heard. Even in what's become a physically difficult walk, she radiates because she's not only alive but also prepared for both tomorrow *and* today. And, as I hear her story and her laughter, I ask myself, "Me too?"

Held by God's Hand

"If I rise on the wings of the dawn, if I settle on the far side of the sea, even there your hand will guide me, your right hand will hold me fast" (Ps. 139:9-10).

Scotty and I would fly over the Atlantic. For me, it would be a first, and I was afraid.

"We'll fly at night, Babe," Scotty said. "You won't even know if we're over water or land."

His attempt to reassure failed. Over land, flight made sense. But over ocean swells taller than a house?

Pressing my forehead against my window, I admitted I could see none of what I feared. But the thought of those icy depths below unnerved me.

For 10 hours, I gripped armrests and consumed quarts of water and Diet Coke in an attempt to deal with what my spouse called "cotton mouth." By the time we reached our destination, I was so exhausted I could barely vacate my seat.

On the return trip, however, something happened to change not only me but also how I felt about flying.

First, the morning sun lit up the Alps, and they were beautiful. The Emerald Isle, to my surprise, really was emerald green. Miniature freighters and passenger-bearing ships appeared to bob along without effort across what looked now to be a tranquil sea. The sapphire North Atlantic glistened. Enormous ice floes looked like works of art. And realizing my Father had created all that my eyes beheld, I thanked Him for yet another adventure, for yet another opportunity to grow. God, the Creator, was with us. There was nothing to fear.

Wonderfully Made

"For you created my inmost being; you knit me together in my mother's womb. I praise you because I am fearfully and wonderfully made; your works are wonderful, I know that full well" (Ps. 139:13-14).

"Rh negative. A fetus two inches longer than average. You're very small to be carrying such a large baby. Its head is too large for its face."

This was my daughter's first baby, my first grandchild. The doctor was suggesting complications, a possible caesarean section, perhaps a problem birth. We wouldn't know until *after* my daughter had entered the delivery room.

Nearing the end of our long-distance call, I heard her imagine the worst. My heart beat like a bird's, while my breathing nearly stopped. We worried aloud, we prayed, and that night, between ugly dreams, I tossed when I should have slept.

The following morning, however, while washing breakfast dishes, I began to recall that Scripture declared we were wonderfully made. The "we" included my grandchild.

"Honey," I told my daughter when she called later that day, "lay your hands on yourself and say aloud for the baby's hearing, 'You are "fearfully and wonderfully made: marvellous are [God's] works, and that my soul knoweth right well!"'" (KJV).

Hanging up, I thought aloud, "And you, Grandma, lay your hands on your fears and praise God. Your grandchild's substance is not hidden from Him."

Then, we waited. Some days, anxious. Other days, calm. But always remembering "fearfully and wonderfully made."

* * *

Yesterday, I took my daughter and my granddaughter to lunch. I'd been busy all morning, hadn't felt like doing my hair, so I'd pulled it back in a gray ponytail.

My daughter would be attending a short meeting before we could eat. I agreed to take Morgan Grace with me.

I parked my car, walked around to the passenger side, and opened the back door. I had just reached in to lift my grandchild up and out of her car seat when she looked up and said, "Hey, what happened to your hair?"

"I just pulled it back today," I said, undoing her safety strap.

"*You* did that?" she asked, a frown on her two-and-a-half-year-old face.

"Yup," I said, smiling. "What's the matter with that?"

She grinned, threw her head back, and lifted her hands to her soft, round cheeks. "It looks goofy, Mom-Mom," she said.

She was right, it did. But as I set her on her feet and took her hand in mine, headed for the Disney Store to buy something before lunch, I didn't care how my hair looked. What mattered to me was that I looked like a grandma walking her hopping, talkative, laughing granddaughter. Yes, she loved to tease, and yes, she was still grinning up into my face and saying something about my looking like Donald Duck, but she was here and healthy and wonderfully made. And, as my grandchild pushed the button for the up elevator, I praised God.

Oh, Boy . . . It's Cold!

I absolutely cannot stand to be cold! Winter mornings, I warm my lingerie and polypropylene socks over kerosene heat. I also ignore my husband's jokes! What does a Montanan know? A man who believes the cold is all in my head?

Earlier, my knees knocking, I'd fondly recalled forced-air heating and thermostats set at 72 degrees. "This is like camping out!" I'd grumbled, inching from under wintry sheets and blankets of wool while my husband happily made his way to the kitchen's kerosene heater with his flashlight in one hand, feeling for the wall—because, at 4:30 A.M., it's more than a little dark.

Kerosene heaters, woodstoves, thermal clothing from L. L. Bean. Never in my goofiest dreams did I imagine that as we "moved up," we'd be roughing it in clothing designed for back woods—donning kneesocks, sweatpants, a flannel gown, and a turtleneck for bed!

"Do you understand what that does to a marriage?" a friend once asked. "Nancy, it's not very romantic, you know."

"Romantic? Where we live?"

Then there's all that wood we have to stack—all the while praying we won't run out and have to come up with an additional $135! The neighbor offered us wood this year, which blessed our pocketbooks! He didn't offer to help us haul and stack. In a delirious moment, *I'd* offered to help my spouse, though. Said, "I'd *like* to help you, Honey." But had I actually said it would be *fun*? Hot chocolate and warm fires and Scrabble with old friends is fun. But wood stacking? "Have a clue!" as my youngest used to say; "be real."

For an hour I pretended business *inside* the house—while my husband began hauling in a wheelbarrow, the first of six cords.

"I'll be there just as soon as I take care of this wash," I periodically chirped from behind priscillas and kitchen panes.

"I'm coming," I promised more than once, wondering if I shouldn't dust lampshades first and check to see that all the lightbulbs were screwed in tight.

My inventions kept me coming up with reasons not to join in on "the fun" for about an hour and a half. Eventually, however, I couldn't face myself. I called out the door that I only had to decide what I'd cook next Saturday "when everyone comes for the chili feed." Then, I'd "be right out."

"Why don't you cook chili?" my husband asked, chuckling, adjusting his seasoned mountain parka and threadbare knit hat.

He was right. I was digging pretty deep now for reasons not to help. So, bundled against bitter winds, I joined my spouse for what a person would think—if they regarded the expression on Scotty's face—was just plain fun.

Within minutes I discovered he'd barely made a dent in the neighbor's stack. It isn't that he works slowly—it's just that he has to stop and study the cardinals, talk to the jays, check to see if there are nuts enough for the squirrels and fresh water that hasn't frozen—in case anyone wants a drink. That he needed my help, in more ways than one, was obvious, if we expected to get the wood stacked before the next predicted storm.

So I stacked wood and tried to keep my nagging to a bare minimum. I remembered aloud natural gas and New Mexico. I recollected sidewalks, warm floors, and fenced backyards. We'd traded all that for garbage that had to be hauled to the road? Newspapers delivered only when the spirit moved some stranger in an unmarked van? A woodstove that belched and stands of split oak where mice erected nests and scared me half out of my wits?

"At least the kerosene heater will feel good," I mumbled, pounding my gloves together, wondering if my fingers would fall off.

Scotty grinned, his mustache frosted and catching the sun. "This is the life, huh, Babe?" He grinned.

Yeh, sure, I thought, some life. By the time the floors had warmed and my fingers had thawed, it would be time to get ready for bed. "I just hope I have extra kneesocks," I grumbled, knowing it would be another one of those nights when I'd warm my night clothes over the stove. "This is the pits," I grumped, and would have said more—but, suddenly, I remembered a man.

He no doubt had a name, but no one seemed to know or care who he was. I'd spotted him the Sunday afternoon Scotty and I had checked into a Holiday Inn in Washington, D.C. He'd set up housekeeping across the street from our showy, fourth-floor retreat. While we tucked ourselves into a king-sized bed, he'd slept on a grate, surrounded by all-night traffic and wind-whipped debris. He fed on scraps from a shopping bag, while we stuffed ourselves in an elegant dining room. He huddled in frayed blankets, while we basked in fresh sheets. He stored all of his worldly belongings in a paper tote, while we'd packed only a sample of ours in luggage trimmed in leather and bearing tags from around the world.

"Yes," I whispered now, touching my husband's parka sleeve, grateful for his ability to provide for his family. "This is the life," I added, noting how content was my rural-loving spouse; noting, too, it had something to do with stacking wood and roughing it and kerosene stoves. "This is the life," I repeated, warming suddenly and noting that a chickadee had begun to sing over sunflower seeds in its simple country shelter out of the cold.

We Give Thanks

Dr. Harold Sala, in a tract titled *Thanksgiving and Praise,* wrote, "You can hang your head in defeat and drag your chin on the ground, or you can lift your heart and voice toward heaven and praise the Lord." I agreed when I first read his comments. I continue to agree. But, in the memory part of me, where I recall that just the two of us have spent more holidays alone together than we have with family, I enter into a debate. I also pray *someone* will come spend the upcoming holiday with us—my oldest with our new grandson in her arms, or my youngest with her toddler tagging along behind. But what if they don't come? What if no one can? What if distance, weather, finances isolate us again? What then? Will I focus on me and mope?

I'm sorry to have to admit that, in the past, I've done a great deal of moping. For a while after my husband's work began to move us from state to state, I couldn't seem to get it through my head *we* were a family—the two of us. Even though we were several thousand miles from the folks we loved so much, we *could* give thanks. I guess, thinking back, living in a caring neighborhood in New

Mexico turned my thinking around—turned it around because, in that community, we discovered friends of the heart—strangers who became family.

In New Mexico we met couples who were either alone together or young families miles from grandparents because job transfers had relocated them. It soon seemed perfectly natural to plan holidays with neighbors, and I began to make myself thank God for whatever setting I found myself in.

I'll admit, at first, I looked to the others to include Scotty and me. We, of course, took dishes—mostly because I feel a part of what's going on when I'm allowed to contribute to the meal. It's difficult for those of us (and our numbers are growing) who've been bounced from one state to the next. We often long for the familiar, especially when it comes to holidays. When I'm invited, I beg the hostess to let me bring shrimp tomato aspic. It's a tradition in the Hoag family. Let me bring the aspic and I'll feel right at home, and so will my spouse.

In New Mexico, many of our friends were parents of preschoolers. I discovered my guests were more relaxed (and more apt to say yes to invitations again) if I made a place and planned for their children—encouraged the parents to bring a child's favorite game or toy.

One year, there were 30 of us sharing turkey and pumpkin pie. In order to fit everyone into our very small house, we had to borrow picnic tables, benches, and chairs. But what a day; what a good memory! One man was trying to deal with a drinking problem; he'd also just recently divorced. He came alone and stayed until everyone else had gone home—and we were able to offer our undivided attention and to share our faith with him. There was also a widow, a young couple who brought baked Alaska, and the mother of a handicapped child who arrived with a fabulous hot crab dip. We'd invited a middle-aged couple, Scotty invited colleagues, I invited a woman from the YWCA. And, that year, we learned about an ice-breaker that, to this day, is tradition at our house—wherever our house happens to be. The icebreaker? Unpopped corn. I place three kernels on every dinner place, and before Scotty asks the blessing, each member of the "family" is invited to name something he or she is thankful for—one blessing for each kernel of corn.

From New Mexico, we moved to Pennsylvania, and I made a new friend of the heart.

When Jane came to dinner, we always asked her to bring her honeyed onions. They were excellent because they were one of Jane's specialties and because she was an excellent cook. She was also the kind of hostess who made everyone feel at home in her home. That's why, one day, I asked what her hospitality secrets were. She shared three.

First, remember when you invite guests, you're actually inviting them to *live* in your home—at least for a short period of time. A house that doesn't look lived in doesn't look as if you're inviting your guests to relax. So, don't fuss so much over how the house looks. Better to concern yourself with how your guests *feel*.

Second, let your guests stir the gravy, chop something, grab the rolls, don an apron, pour the coffee or tea . . .

Third? Try to get most of the work out of the way *before* your company arrives. Then you'll have lots of time to mingle, to make your new friends comfortable.

Yes, there are still those special times of the year when no one's available, when it's just my husband and me in some "foreign" restaurant in a new town. One year, bless his heart, Scotty tried to make up for the newness and for there being no children to help us celebrate. He tried by making reservations at an inn with violins and guitars and a banqueting table replete with pheasant under glass. But the day didn't go well. And, later, I knew why—knew that only when I look beyond myself and do my level best either to invite others who will be alone or visit someone shut in does it become a memorable and happy holiday. This is not my nature—looking out for others. But God has been patient with me. In fact, some holidays, I've actually wondered if it's His loving patience that has separated me from the familiar that I might learn how good it can be to reach out.

Billy Graham, in *Christian Herald,* November/December 1989, wrote, "God has given us two hands—one to receive with and the other to give with."

Finally, after what for a while seemed just too many holidays away from home, I've learned to say, "Amen."

Who May Stand There?

"Who may ascend the hill of the Lord? Who may stand in his holy place?" (Ps. 24:3).

The first summer our granddaughter came to visit us, she was just 16 months old—full of delight and curiosity! And between the neighbor's house and ours, she discovered a slope so gentle adults might easily miss it. Her cheeks fresh, her jacket only half-zipped, and her blond curls dancing, she'd squeeze my hand tight and lead me—all the while grinning—and down the hill we'd "race." Both laughing, both singing, "Whee, whee . . ."

This morning as I read the 24th psalm, I remember not only Morgan Grace's visit but that God said He desired that we come to Him as little children too.

Who may ascend His hill? Only children—those who have clean hands, hands that have been offered to the

Lord to be cleansed, hands that cling to Him. He delights in children with pure hearts, hearts that trust Him as my grandchild trusted me; children who put God first, children who are not self-impressed, children who are grateful for simple pleasures provided by a loving Father God. He looks for children who are open, who don't set out to deceive or to proclaim what is false—a generation of children who will joyfully seek His face.

His heart finds pleasure in children, like Morgan Grace, who will put their hand in His and exclaim, "Whee . . ."

The Automatic Pilot

"If you'll just hook your seat belts," someone announced, "we're about to arrive in Seattle."

I touched my nose to the window. All I could see was fog and an occasional glimpse of earth. How could the pilot be so certain Sea-Tac airstrips were directly below?

My hands began to feel sticky and damp. I drew my upper lip between my teeth. Would there be bumps in the runway? Would our landing upset my stomach so that I'd be less than what my daughter needed? When she met me at the gate, she expected me to be coolheaded and strong. I envisioned my becoming ill.

It's not that I'm afraid to fly, but given a choice I'll go by train. However, when Lisa called, I heard what she did not say. I heard it was urgent—that she needed me *now*. A midnight flight would be a must. Because my thoughts were on my fledgling and not on my phobia, I'd thrown clothing into an overnight tote, dashed to the airport, paid for the ticket, and boarded with the crowd. Not until morning—and after an entire night's sleepless travel—did I begin to consider my being midair and whether or not our landing would go well.

Swallowing audibly, I recalled, "Now faith is being sure of what we hope for and certain of what we do not see" (Heb. 11:1). I couldn't see the wheels drop, but I felt them chunk into place, and I wondered if they had touched down on level ground.

My husband had prayed with me just before I'd departed, but sitting tense now and with my heels pressed tight against the aircraft's floor, I whispered a prayer of my own. It was not exactly the sort you'd offer out loud with others listening, but prayer. I also remembered that just the day before—worried about my daughter and fearing I wouldn't be able to meet her needs—I'd read, "Be strong and of good courage; . . . for the Lord your God is with you wherever you go" (Josh. 1:9, RSV).

I buckled my belt, folded my hands in my lap, blinked rapid flutters to dam tears, and murmured a hope He was here.

Soon, we began to brake. I pressed my head into the starched, white cloth behind me. Pavement touched rubber; we'd landed, and my stomach was still in place. And beyond my window, I glimpsed the tip of Mount Rainier.

"That was the nicest landing I've ever experienced," I said to the passenger sitting on the aisle. I should tell the stewardess or pilot, I thought. But I'd no sooner made a move to deplane—rehearsing all the while the congratulations I'd offer—when a male voice broke in.

"Well, folks, I certainly hope you enjoyed that. And, for those of you who don't fly often, thought you'd like to know the smooth landing you just experienced was all executed by the automatic pilot."

There was more explanation, but most of it went by me as I tried to take in what I had heard: an automatic pilot figured the speed, the wind, whether or not the weather was in the way? An unruffled aviator had controlled the approach and ignored the dense fog.

Moving toward the terminal and a daughter who would need my best, I thought, Wouldn't all of my journeys go better, airborne or earthbound, if I'd take my hands off the controls?

Stepping from the baggage claim area and into the gleaming, noise-filled lobby, I spotted my youngest: bundled against the cold, hair in a ponytail, questions written across her face.

I smiled, knowing I would soon tell her, "You're in expert hands, Honey. We both are. We have nothing to fear. We'll simply leave the navigating to our Automatic Pilot. Then both the passage and the landing will be good."

Dealing with Divorce

One morning I was sitting on our patio watching the young man next door. Only days before, his wife had left him. She'd found someone else. It was obvious he was having a difficult time knowing how to function, how to live with seeing his children only once a week.

The young husband-father is a Christian, but he's faltering. He has dropped out of church. There's no doubt in my mind he loves the Lord—but he loved his wife and children too. And today, prayer and gatherings down at the church don't seem enough. He's angry, he's in pain. He wants to hit back, take it out on someone.

I understand where our neighbor is. It took me years to get over my own divorce, to feel the questions had been answered, to stop hating the others, to stop tormenting myself. Like my neighbor friend, I didn't walk through my divorce with style and grace. I also lashed out, behaved badly, presented a pretty awful example of what it meant to be Christlike.

In my opinion, divorce is a weak prescription for a dreadful sickness in the house. When I divorced, it divided my kids. Two elected to go with their father and his new wife; the youngest chose to live with me, to tough it out while I waited tables and worked on a master's degree. Waiting tables isn't easy. What made it worse was hearing through the grapevine I wasn't "much of a mother" out working when I should have been home.

I remember one woman. "God *hates* divorce," she said, drawing herself up straight to tower over me.

"Yes, I know," I said. "He hates judging too."

No, comeback wasn't exactly Christian, but in those days, I didn't feel Christian. I felt alone.

One day, with doubt and fear and a problem budget tormenting me, I decided we needed a church. I dressed my little girl "to the teeth"—and I dressed up too. We held hands, imagined a grandmother who'd invite us home for dinner, walked in, sat down, sang, listened, prayed, and walked out. No one had spoken to us. No one.

When I was a child, I remember chicken pox. The doctor said the pox would itch. He wasn't telling me anything I didn't already know. Mother said, "Don't scratch. It will hurt." I knew that too. The divorced who are behaving badly? They know.

Divorce is a death in the family without the flowers, the hot dishes, the condolences, the support.

Divorcées often blame God. We ask, "Why?" We wonder how it was He allowed us to marry in the first place. And where was He when we were hurting so and our brothers and sisters were taking potshots at us? If there is a God, why can't He make everything better? We need friends to come alongside—to walk a while with us.

It took me a number of years before I would go back to the church. Only after I'd met and married a Christian man did I decide to give it another try. While I'd cut off the Christian community, I hadn't quit God. I'd only rejected the people who'd claimed to be His but who hadn't represented Him very well.

Today, I think about my neighbor, and I realize I haven't prayed for him much. Mostly, I've noted his hurt and remembered my own. Because his parents are standing with him, I suppose I decided he didn't actually need anything I could offer him. But, truth is, he needs someone to pray, and I can do that.

As I consider how good God's been to me and how happily married I am today, I'm reminded to encourage those of you who've either recently divorced or who haven't yet healed. God hasn't forsaken you. You may not feel like looking to Him for help right now, but you can count on it: no matter where you are on the journey, He has His eye on you. He's waiting because He loves you, and when you're ready for Him to do so, He's going to make your life good again.

He can. And He will.

Time Out!

The minute the lights dim I know: we're going to lose our electricity *again*. Howling winds have kicked up. Trees are yielding branches and leaves. Torrential rains, like toy soldiers with snare drums, parade across the windowpanes. And the house grows still.

"Hooray!" I cheer. We'll dine by candlelight, play a table game over coffee, communicate.

But first, I'll check the kerosene heaters and make certain they're full. If I wait until Scotty comes home, it'll be almost too dark to find the garage, let alone the five-gallon cans.

We'll need the woodstove cranked up, too, if the storm lingers, and from the looks of things, that's exactly what it's going to do.

Hauling wood is fun, I secretly admit. "Amazing," I say, "how I'm adjusting to life without sidewalks and corner drugstores."

After the stove and heaters, I locate candles—collect a cluster in the middle of the pine kitchen table and group several in both our bedroom and bath.

"How romantic the house looks," I brag aloud. Maybe I'll slip into something comfortable. I glance at the thermometer attached to the back door. "Twenty degrees!" Something comfortable, I decide, will be my long underwear.

Soon I also locate batteries and, on a portable radio, discover soothing gospel music and a jovial preacher's voice. Suddenly, I'm in no hurry to be anywhere, get anything done. A sweet, slow pace seems to envelop the house, and I, normally a wood bee preparing for fall, relax. Usually I'm complaining, "Where does the time go?" But, now, all electric clocks are motionless. Even my watch hands seem barely to move. After dinner, we'll read by the fire. Abraham Lincoln would feel right at home.

I don a down sweater and a second pair of socks while the woods and thickets hum with birdcalls out back.

A neighbor friend phones to say there's a fir across the main road and power lines. It may be hours. All commuters are being turned back.

Outdoors, I spot flares and drivers backing in a fury

up the road. I phone Scotty, tell him to please be careful driving home.

"Yes, Mommy," he says, chuckling. Will I never change?

"Probably not," I say.

The storm withdraws. I don a mackinaw and head for our driveway to catch a sunset above the hills beyond a farm. I wonder when I last felt I had the time to savor such things.

Peach, pink, and mauve play across the sky and tint our windows upstairs. I stand with my hands in my pockets—going nowhere—feeling there's nothing I *have to* do. The sky's pumpkin now, with a glimmer of lavender blue framing evergreen silhouettes—and I remember being a child, lying on my back in sweet-smelling grass, tracing elephants and angels in the clouds.

I also remember the birds. This storm hit right at feeding time. I take out an extra can of sunflower seeds. Come daybreak, there will be second helpings for everyone.

We may be without power until morning, Scotty informs, sloshing through the basement door and shaking rain from his coat, imitating the neighbor's black Lab.

"Shopping centers were hit too," he says. "Repairmen will see to businesses first. How big a deal do you suppose a dozen houses are to the electric company?" he asks.

"I don't care," I say—more content than I've felt in months.

We opt for a soup supper heated on the woodstove. After a dessert of chocolate mints, a Christmas gift from my firstborn, we play a game and heat hand-ground coffee over kerosene.

"Romantic," I whisper, snuggling close to my mate.

"Don't flush the toilets, Babe," Scotty says—reminding me the well's on an electric pump.

OK, so it's not exactly the evening I envisioned. But it

still beats television—no gruesome news. I pretend we're pioneers as we add an extra wool blanket to the bed.

Not until the following morning do I begin to think enough is enough. I haven't showered; I have only sufficient water to brush my teeth. My spouse announces he can't stay home for cheese, crackers, and Monopoly. Friends telephone; would we like to take showers at their place? Scotty will. I will not. *How embarrassing.*

Scotty deserts; I find letters that need answering—tug my chair closer to the kerosene heat.

Outside, the sun warms the feeder, and 50 or more birds begin to congregate. Cardinals, chickadees, flickers, jays, a Carolina wren.

I've run out of reheated coffee. I won't go to the store without my hair washed and arranged. I'm becoming grumpy. I'm glad—for Scotty's sake—he's in hot water somewhere else.

I find some spice tea, also a gift from my eldest. I picture civilized Seattle, imagine gentle waves lapping Puget Sound shores.

The tea helps a little, but suddenly I have things to do and places to go. "Get me out of here!" I shout—and the refrigerator groans.

I cheer as our aging appliance shudders, huffs, whirs.

I spot a light in the hallway; the coffeemaker's blue clock begins to blink.

"Electricity!" I rejoice on my way to shower, hoping the water's warm. "It's been real and it's been fun, but it hasn't been *real* fun!" I sing. But, then, I catch a glimpse of sparrows and a dove who's gleaning seeds from below the feeder box. I remember the sunset's extravagant display—know, if I'm wise, I'll catch another tonight—and I amend my former refrain.

"It's been real—the candle glow, the warm fires. It's been fun—the sharing, the Monopoly. It's even been real fun—not caring a whit about where the time's gone." And I thank God for what, at first, looked like catastrophe, but for what became, instead, a blessed "time out."

God of Awesome Deeds

A job promotion had taken us to Pennsylvania, but interest rates were 17 percent and our future was looking grim. Would we find a house with payments we could afford? Our daughter was entering her senior year in high school, our relocation had upset her enough—she didn't need to hear we had no place to live.

Then, one morning after a distressing house-hunting week, our realtor's partner mentioned a place. We drove across town; and we knew, we sensed, God was doing the leading, and this could be the perfect solution for us. But there was one snag: what would they say to so many dollars below their asking price? Yes, the house had been vacant for months because the owners had taken work out of state, but the husband had threatened other realtors and other buyers who had asked him to take less. Still, the couple did "just happen" to be in town that day, and though our realtor wasn't up to facing the man, the owner of the agency had agreed to see what he could do.

At midnight the phone rang in our motel room. Our prayers had been answered—our offer accepted—but the most exciting part of the whole event we didn't hear until the following day when we met with our realtor's boss.

"The owner was furious!" he said. "But after hours of *discussion*, all of a sudden the wife walked in and announced, 'I know you don't want to sell, but for whatever reason, God wants *this* couple to have *this* house.'"

It was settled, and for seven years that house was ours.

Cleansed by Faith

Head bowed, her shoulders dipped, the young woman sat on our sofa and wept.

I remembered her with my youngest—cheering football teams and winning a spot on homecoming court. She was always smiling, seemingly delighted with life.

But today she'd come to share heartbreaking stories and tears. She hadn't been happy; she'd been abused. She hadn't been hopeful; she'd attempted to take her own life.

Yes, she'd accepted Jesus as her Savior, but now she believed she had to *do* something to keep His love—to receive forgiveness for having responded in kind to a lifestyle that had been cruel and base.

"I make promises but I foul up," she said. "I promise Him I'll fast for a month, give up sweets, never lie, go see my mother, change the way I dress. Then I turn around and do something stupid again."

"What about plain and simple faith?" I asked.

"I've got to *do* something . . . to feel clean . . . don't I?"

"You've turned your life over to Him. Right?"

"Right."

"Then why work so hard trying to persuade Him? He's already decided; He loves you. All He asks for is your trust."

"That's it?" my visitor asked.

"Nothing else."

My visitor smiled a child's smile; and, remembering I had also been forgiven, I smiled too.

God's Still Calling

"Then Eli realized that the Lord was calling the boy" (1 Sam. 3:8).

"Honestly, I don't know about you. You're out of one thing and into another. Teaching, Tupperware, secretary, waitress, and delivering papers. What exactly do you want to be when you grow up?"

My friend's question seemed inappropriate. When I grow up? I was middle-aged! Truth was, though, I didn't have an answer. I'd tried to return to the classroom, picked up odd jobs. I thought I wanted to be a writer, but even that wasn't going well. "A writer? Where do you get such notions?" a relative asked.

Embarrassed, I mumbled something and let the subject drop. Just because Anne had become an artist, Shirley was designing jewelry, Bev had found her niche in Little Theatre, a neighbor had opened her own cafe . . .

Well, maybe I *was* foolish. After all, weren't writers different? odd? Not until I met Donna did I understand I would find no peace until I listened to what my heart was telling me.

"I need to talk to you," she said. What she told me I'll never forget.

"Nancy, when you wonder about writing, I believe you're hearing the Lord. Last night, I *know* He awakened me, and I'm certain I'm to pass this along." She held out a note she'd penned in the middle of the night, a confirmation. I had heard the Lord, I was learning to recognize His voice.

I believe we are all called—some to homemaking, some to working out, some to raising children, others to writing books. We may be called to serve family, we may be called to paint, to manage a government agency, to counsel, to sculpt, to teach.

Each of us is unique, but we all have this one thing in common: we were gifted by our Father with a specific purpose in mind. God's still calling. We can learn to listen—or we can choose not to hear Him—and miss it all.

Uprooted Again?

My husband's work had again relocated us. This move had supposedly been an answer to our prayers. We'd moved west—to the place we called home. But we'd only begun to unpack when our daughter decided to marry back east; we'd hoped she'd be joining *us*. Before long, a grandchild was on the way. Our daughter would definitely be staying put now, and I wondered what we were doing in the wild West!

"This moving around is so hard!" I cried, wanting my husband to make everything better, knowing there wasn't a thing he could do. I needed friends, family, roots. I was beginning already to hate the frozen land, the winter sky, towering mountain peaks.

I'd barely adjusted to my daughter's decisions when my son wrote from New York to say he wanted nothing more to do with us. He'd embraced New Age, said Christians were the reason there was no peace in the world. Scotty wasn't certain his new job was all that he wanted or needed at this point in his career. And I began to grieve. I needed my prayer partner, but even she lived on the East Coast. Scotty tried comforting me; a new acquaintance gave me a pocket calendar that declared, "Resolve to keep happy." But I doubted I had an ounce of resolve left.

According to recent reports, next to death and divorce, a move is the most stressful thing that can happen to you—especially when coupled with a job transfer into a new community. Studies have come up with a list of the 10 most stressful things that lead to ill health: a major move is number three. The family member most apt to feel the strain? The spouse, usually the female, tops the list. For the next year I, the female spouse, would spend a great deal of time in my bathrobe, wonder if God was punishing me, learn how to become content.

Reaching out and fitting in isn't easy when it's just your spouse and middle-aged you. There had to be other Christian women in the neighborhood; maybe there were even other depressed wives who needed to talk. But the depression became so heavy I didn't think I could pick up the phone.

I'd told my East Coast friends the West was "heaven on earth." But heaven's temperatures had plummeted below what I believed I could stand.

My former prayer partner called. "What's happened to that faith you're always bragging about?" she asked. "Didn't *you* tell *me* how many times the Lord has seen you through other moves?"

She was right, but I'd lived in seven homes in 15 years in four dissimilar regions of the United States. "Most of us live today in a world of strangers," I'd read. It was true—nothing but strangers on our road, and because I was the one depressed, I refused to turn a one of them into a friend. I'd withdraw to my room in the attic, read letters from friendly neighborhoods, pray for a transfer to where I would be much happier.

One Sunday, however, the local newspaper carried an announcement—something about a Christian women's meeting coming up soon. Visitors were welcome. Scotty coaxed. I balked. He promised dinner out. I said I'd go, and the following Tuesday when I returned home from the luncheon with telephone numbers of new friends, my surroundings began to look just a little better to me. I'd been hugged and I'd agreed to come again.

Several days later, a woman called, said her husband worked with mine. Would I like to come for coffee? "Meet a couple of gals?"

"Would I?" How long would it take me to put on my coat?

Over coffee, I met another woman, Teri, who was also down. Our husbands had relocated at about the same time. Teri introduced me to Christy—also new in town, also living in a motel, also running up telephone bills from $150 to $250 a month, also threatening to join the French foreign legion! *Anything* to escape her 10' x 10' room!

Christy saved my life. "I can tell you when the depression hit," she said, "but I can't tell you when I was all of a sudden well." She said she'd cried at a bank, had to leave running because she'd glanced at her calendar and realized her girlfriends back home would be meeting for breakfast that day.

"I'd walk up to grocery store clerks," she said, "and I'd think, I don't know *you*." Even today the word *move* triggers a panic attack, though she's making what she refers to as her "now friends."

"I wish someone had told me I would one day be better," she said.

I prayed a silent thanks that someone was telling me.

"You need to become involved with Newcomers," Teri and Christy chorused. "All women, all transients." They laughed. Newcomers met for lunch, fashion shows, crafts.

A fourth wife joined us—one who'd been pining away

in a motel room along with her three heirs and a cat—waiting for a "real home."

Minutes into our conversation, our foursome began sharing fears, frustrations, *and* laughter. We decided we would *choose* a new outlook, stop whining about the way things used to be, accept the fact that life and change are synonymous.

We decided to form a club for wives who needed to know who gave puppy shots, when children registered for school, how often garbage was picked up, and where to buy groceries. We began with the four of us, but soon there were others—all needing to plug in somewhere.

Next, I joined Newcomers, tried out for Sweet Adelines, found a church, put together a Writers' Fellowship.

Depression had shut me down, but once I decided not only to join other women for coffee and lunch but also to change how I looked at my circumstances, it began to lift. I admitted I was angry—not only about the moves but at God. My honesty with Him freed me to be honest with myself and to accept responsibility for my moods.

I asked myself what else I could do. I could hope for another transfer for my spouse—one that might put me next door to children and old friends. But was that God's best? The next step became instantly obvious: I needed to pray.

I didn't always feel like praying. But a friend had reminded: If we will use our mouths to pray and to praise—even in the pits—our hearts *will* catch up.

No, I'm still not exactly enamored with this picking up and going down the road. But because God is faithful, I've discovered—even in houses that have turned out not to feel exactly like home—I have roots.

No matter where our husband's occupations take us, we *can* do more than cope; we can become "content . . . in whatsoever state" (Phil. 4:11, KJV).

We can.

Yet . . .

"Yet he saved them for his name's sake, to make his mighty power known" (Ps. 106:8).

"Yet." Just a little word? only three letters long? Not to me it isn't. "Yet" for me represents God's grace, God's love, my mistakes, my failures—examined by a just God, dealt with, and covered by the mighty power that belongs only to Him.

"Yet" means there is One greater than my sins—greater than the one who tempts me to walk in a way displeasing to God, tempts me to anger, tempts me to bear grudges, to seek retribution, to file charges against someone I've decided "did me wrong."

"Yet" means Satan is defeated, God wins! A life that might have otherwise been wasted can go on to glorify God.

"Yet" means at any time, in any place I can drop to my knees and ask His forgiveness and know I have been received.

"Yet" means I can begin again.

Storms Pass, so Hang On!

My husband and his brother had pulled out early in the morning, trusting the skiing would be good and hoping the frequently fickle weather would cooperate. I had decided to stay home, to work, read, and set goals because tomorrow we would open our eyes to a brand-new year.

I looked forward to the New Year, a fresh start. This

last one hadn't gone very well. There'd been a painful estrangement from my son. My youngest, married just a year and now with a brand-new baby, struggled with change and too little money to make ends meet. My husband, who'd prayed and applied for his present position, was questioning his decision—talking about our doing something else. We'd been here before—staying, moving, moving again. What if I couldn't do it this time? I'd already wondered if I'd made one move too many. I was in trouble this time and couldn't seem to snap back. Then, my grandmother died. And, in one week, a member of the family would be filing for divorce.

"What I need today," I said, "is a little quiet and space."

Scotty understood. He'd packed his lunch and his brother's, and soon they were off to the ski hill, while I'd retreated to my office up under the eaves.

Sitting quiet in my wicker chair, I recalled all the promises I'd made to myself about not giving in to depressions. *You've worked this out before; you can do it again.* Hadn't God been faithful? Hadn't He seen me through other seasons when I'd considered giving up?

The answer to both questions was yes: yes, He was faithful; and yes, just about the time I thought I couldn't cope, I'd rediscovered life was good—clouds had lifted, and the sun had come out.

But now—in my retreat—I'd spotted an evil-looking, foreboding fog that had bumped against the mountain to creep over, down, and across the snow-packed peaks and runs. No ,doubt, my skier would be hitting the slopes about now; and because I've been there, I knew he must be thinking the entire Rocky Mountain Range had been swallowed up. Maybe he was also thinking he should just head for home. The wind would be whipping, the quarreling gusts biting and blue-nose cold.

From my window, the mountains seemed close enough to touch. I longed to throw open the sash, to call to my skier-husband as I'd once called to my children when they were about the business of playing in the dark. I would tell him, "Don't quit!" Don't quit, I told myself. "A blue sky is sweeping in behind the heaviness that seems to have wholly taken over and ruined what was to have been your day." "This is the day which the Lord hath made" (Ps. 118:24, KJV). I would tell him that soon he'd be warmed and that the snow would once again glisten and dance in great plumes of crystal-like trinkets as he soared down one experts' run and then the next.

I drew my knees up, laid my head back on my chair. And, what about me? Wasn't I becoming an expert at making familiar runs? Wouldn't I also soar—if I just hung on?

Life is like that. It bumps up against us like winter's clouds—sick babies, an angry son, disillusionment, depression, divorce. But, just as my spouse has skied other days in bitter weather and learned to wait it out, so would I keep going—to see, in due season, the sun shine again.

And what about you? You who've been buffeted by what you can't seem to do a thing about? Those of you who've about decided to give up? To you, I open my window and call, "Hang on! Be strong! Be courageous! Storms last for such a little while, and then . . ."

Also by Nancy Hoag . . .

Good Morning! Isn't It a Fabulous Day!
Parables for Wives and Mothers
BF083-411-3546

Through all the perplexities and pinches of life—"God is here with us, and with Him, it is fabulous!"